Spain
East Coast
From Tarragona to the Costa de Almería

Jarrold Publishing

CONTENTS

Essential details in brief

Name: Reino de España (Kingdom of Spain).

Founded: In 1469, as a result of the marriage between the heirs to the kingdoms of Aragón and Castile.

Form of government: Constitutional monarchy based on a parliamentary democracy. Head of state: King Juan Carlos I. The state parliament consists of two chambers, the Congress with 350 representatives and the Senate with 253 Senators. Both are elected for a period of four years. The present constitution came into force on December 7th 1978. Since the autumn of 1982 the Socialist Party (PSOE) has ruled with an absolute majority.

Administration: 17 autonomous regions.

Languages: In addition to the official language of Spanish, the following languages enjoy equal rights in the corresponding regions. In Galicia, in north-west Spain, Galician, a language similar to Portuguese, is spoken. Basque is spoken in the region of the same name. On the east coast, Catalan and Valencian, both of which are related to the Provençal language of the adjoining south of France, are spoken.

Religion: Almost exclusively Roman Catholic.

Population: 37.68 million.

Capital: Madrid, with a population of approximately 5 million.

Area: 504,811 sq.km divided up as follows. The mainland, 492,265 sq.km. The Balearic Islands, 5014 sq.km. The Canary Islands, 7500 sq.km. Ceuta and Malilla as well as four further coastal settlements in northern Morocco, 32 sq.km. Spain wishes to reclaim the British Crown Colony of Gibraltar which covers an area of 6 sq.km.

Tourism: In 1983, the total number of foreign visitors to Spain was 41 million of whom roughly ¾ were tourists. Income from the tourist industry in 1983 was £5,200 million.

Natural resources: Iron, copper, lead, zinc, manganese, tin, potash, coal. There is hardly any oil.

Important exports: Agricultural products (fruit, oil & wine). Cars (mostly Fords and other foreign makes), steel, shoes and cement.

Vital imports: Crude oil, meat, maize, oil-seeds and machinery.

...y of life

...anges have been taking place in Spanish society over the last fifteen ...age of a very conservative, Catholic and patriarchal community is not a ...ore, at least not in the larger towns. There are in Spain today two very ...ways of life. There is that of the middle-class citizens living in the developed ...and cities, and there is also that of the country-dwellers in the small rural or ...vincial townships. And yet much that can be described as typically Spanish applies to both. Family life always plays a very important role and a close bond exists among the members of a family. Elderly parents usually live with one of their children as the idea of an old people's home is, to a Spaniard, horrific. Since divorce became legal in Spain all the experts have waited for a great increase in the number of separations — but it has not happened.

As in Italy little children are idolised. They always appear to be with their families, whether it be for an outing in the evening or perhaps going to church. On the other hand, parents who live in the country expect that when their children leave school at the age of fourteen they will find work and contribute to the support of the family. The surprisingly low illiteracy rate of 8% shows that children have had at least some formal education.

The majority of Spanish adult women are housewives. Most husbands want to remain the sole bread-winners and it is only when the wage is not sufficient to maintain the family that they allow the lady of the house to seek work. And what is the daily routine of the families represented here? It is somewhat different from ours. The first breakfast consists usually of a croissant, coffee and cognac, or an aniseed liqueur for the men. At 11 a.m. they have a substantial breakfast with eggs and sausage, and coffee, beer or wine. Lunch, which consists of several courses, is taken at about 3 in the afternoon. At 7 or 8 p.m. they have a snack and at about 11 p.m. a light supper is served. You can now fully appreciate why Spanish women have a tendency to become plump!

Do not be put off by the noise, for Spaniards talk loudly and furiously. In addition they are born actors, so that even the most commonplace matters soon become the subject of hot debate. The speed of delivery of the Spanish language enhances this effect. Just a brief word on the proverbial pride of the Spanish people, as it really does exist. The Spaniard is proud of practically everything which concerns him personally and is particularly sensitive when criticised for it. This feeling of personal honour is one of the most charming qualities of the national character. A Spaniard does not feel inferior to anybody else and because of that everyone is treated with exactly the same courtesy.

How the Spanish make a living

People are often inclined to think that life in the Mediterranean areas revolves around olive trees, grapevines and the tourist industry. Posters issued by government tourist offices are frequently responsible for this idyllic but mistaken assumption. They depict contented old men driving their donkeys along dusty roads under the blazing noon-day sun. This is not always the case, however, especially in Spain. Tourism does indeed play an important role. Each year some 40 million people visit the country, which itself has a population of only 38 million. But apart from that Spain is an industrial nation striving for progress, with all the attendant internal upheaval

Olives and vines, Poblet

which that involves. With its gross national product, Spain occupies 11th position in the league table of industrial nations. In some spheres productivity is quite surprising. In fact the motor manufacturers are producing almost as many vehicles per year as those in Britain. The products of the Spanish aeronautical industry are highly regarded (small propellered aircraft for internal air services), as are those of the arms industry which always sell well in Third World countries. The rifles and pistols which are manufactured in the Basque region have a worldwide reputation. In addition there are of course those agricultural products which have become proverbial: wine, olive oil and citrus fruits.

In spite of attempts at decentralisation, heavy industry is still concentrated in and around Madrid, Barcelona and the Basque country. The majority of people are employed in the service sector which includes the tourist trade. On the east coast agriculture plays a very important part. Citrus fruits are grown here, while Murcia and Valencia are the largest rice-growing regions in Europe. About a quarter of the working population is employed in agriculture; in Almería with its acres of spring vegetables the proportion reaches 40%. The fact that so many people still work on the land is partly explained by the way the terrain is divided up. In this corner of Spain there are very few large estates but a great number of smallholdings, which often keep the whole family busy.

This chequered nature of the countryside in southern Valencia is made even more colourful by the existence of many centuries-old traditional cottage industries which abound in Alicante province. Whole villages specialise in a particular product and have become leaders in their field. If it should become necessary, however, they are quite capable of switching quickly to something new in the way that certain villages in the region, which had for centuries been the leading producers of saffron, acted when a better and cheaper crop was produced elsewhere. They bought up the harvest of their rivals and concentrated on processing the raw material. A substantial part of the toy industry has become established around Alicante, while glassware, shoes, carpets and confectionery are made in the region. One village makes dolls' eyes of different types and sizes which are exported to Japan.

The standard of living has risen by leaps and bounds in the last thirty years. The average annual income is very much higher than in the other 'poor' Mediterranean countries such as Yugoslavia, Greece and Turkey.

🦅 Signposts of History

12th to 6th c. B.C: Phoenicians and Greeks settle on the Iberian coast.

238 B.C: The Carthaginians invade the Iberian Peninsula and, under Hamilcar, begin the colonisation of the Mediterranean coast.

218–201 B.C: In the 2nd Punic War the Carthaginians under Hannibal are defeated by the Romans and Spain becomes a Roman province.

A.D. 414: Germanic peoples invade.

5th c. A.D: The Visigoths establish their kingdom with its capital at Toledo.

A.D. 711: Invasion by the Moors. Under Tarik, the Arabs cross the Straits of Gibraltar, defeat the Goths, and conquer the whole of Spain.

8th to 15th c: Moorish rule in Spain, at first as far north as the Pyrenees, but later only in the south and mostly in the form of small principalities quarrelling with one another. In the north Christian kingdoms become established and form alliances for the purpose of the reconquest (Reconquista) of the Arab regions.

1094–1100: El Cid conquers Valencia and holds it for a short time.

1238: Final conquest of Valencia by King James I of Aragón.

13th to 15th c: The golden age of Aragón. From their capital at Zaragoza its kings also reign over Catalonia, Valencia, the Balearic Islands, Sardinia, Naples and parts of Greece.

1479: Christian Spain is united under one ruler as a result of the marriage between Isabella of Castile and Ferdinand of Aragón.

1492: The Moors are expelled from Spain with the fall of Granada, their last capital city, and the whole of Spain is under Christian rule. At the same time America is discovered and Spain becomes a world power.

1517–1700: Rule of the Habsburgs.

1609: Expulsion of 300,000 Moors. The Spanish economy is shattered.

1700–1714: The War of the Spanish Succession places a French Bourbon prince on the throne of Spain.

1707: Aragón, Valencia and Catalonia all lose their autonomy as a result of the policy of centralisation adopted by the Bourbons.

18th c: Close ties between Spain and France, by means of the 'family pact' which Napoleon uses to his advantage.

1808–1814: Napoleon places his brother Joseph on the Spanish throne and the outraged Spaniards revolt. Aided by the British they succeed in freeing the country from Napoleonic rule in the Peninsular War. Severe devastation.

19th c: Revolts in almost all the American colonies together with discord in the House of Bourbon which is once more in power. Armed uprisings and civil war. Spain no longer has the strength to maintain its position as a world power.

1868–1874: The height of disorder. Queen Isabella II is banished. The House of Savoy attempts to rule but fails. The country becomes a republic and finally the House of Bourbon returns.

1898: War with America. Loss of Spain's last colonies, the Philippines, Cuba and Puerto Rico. The end of Spanish rule overseas.

1923–1930: Dictatorship under General Primo de Rivera.

1931: Governmental crises and dissatisfaction among the people compel King Alfonso XIII to flee the country and the 2nd Republic is proclaimed.

1936–1939: Mounting crises and political radicalisation split the country in two. The revolt of General Franco and his army brings about Civil War. This bitter and ruthless struggle shakes the whole world.

1939–1975: Authoritarian regime of General Franco.

Since 1975: Constitutional monarchy under King Juan Carlos I in accordance with the constitution of 1978.

Phases of History

Invasions

Spanish history begins with the arrival on her shores of foreign invaders. The first to settle were the Phoenicians. They founded Cádiz, the largest city in Europe at that period. With the Phoenicians came the first Jewish immigrants, who were to play a very important role in Spain. There then followed the Greeks who concentrated their settlements on the Mediterranean coast. It was now the turn of the Carthaginians who made Nova Carthago, known today as Cartagena, the centre of their colony in Spain. In the 3rd century B.C., the Romans appeared and drove the Carthaginians out of Spain in the course of three Punic Wars in 264–241, 218–201, and 149–146 B.C.

All these invaders encountered the indigenous Iberians whose origins are not known. The most recent archaeological finds and indications lead the experts to believe that these people had occupied the east coast around Valencia since the dawn of history, and in fact it is even possible that the area may prove to have been the cradle of Eurasian man. The Celts who came from north of the Pyrenees joined up with the native Iberians to form a primitive but by no means an untalented race. The world-famous sculpture of the 'Lady of Elche', so called after the place where it was found, is proof that they knew how to assimilate the knowledge and arts of the invader, in this case the Greeks, without losing any of their own originality.

Spain became Latinised under Roman rule and Rome was so closely linked to its Iberian provinces that many Spaniards achieved high status. The Emperors Trajan, Hadrian and Marcus Aurelius as well as the writers Seneca, Martial and Lucan were all Spaniards. The Pax Romana lasted until the beginning of the 5th century A.D. when the Visigoths invaded the country from southern France. Rome no longer had the power to resist them and for almost three centuries Spain was ruled from Toledo by the elected kings of the Visigoths. It was during this period that the Christianisation of the country, which had begun under the Romans, greatly increased.

The Moors

In the year A.D. 711 the invasion from the south took place. The North African Berber general Tarik, in the service of the Caliph of Damascus, crossed from the place now known as Morocco over the straits which have since been named after him, for Gibraltar is derived from the Arabic for the Rock of Tarik. At one stroke, the Arabs conquered almost the whole of Spain, only the extreme north putting up any resistance, and it was there that the Christian prince Pelayo inflicted the first defeat upon them. Shortly afterwards they abandoned all further attempts to obtain a foothold in France when Charles Martel, the grandfather of Charlemagne, struck them a crushing blow at Poitiers. As a result of this defeat the Arabs gave up all thoughts of further expansion in Europe and, retreating to the Pyrenees, they finally halted the advancing Christian army and established their northern borders there.

In Córdoba, their capital, they developed a way of life which greatly impressed Christian visitors. Its splendour was unprecedented and its arts, manual skills and learning were on a level far superior to that of Christian Europe. The court library, for instance, contained 600,000 books. In addition the Arabs were excellent soldiers, whose weapons filled their opponents with envy. At that time, many Christian princes ordered their weaponry from Córdoba, as well as silk, linen and cottons for their wives and daughters. The doctor, too, was always summoned from that city, as were private tutors for the sons of the family.

Tolerance and development

The Moors cannot take full credit for the splendour which they developed, as the Christians and the Jews also played a very important role. Thanks to the tolerance which was one of the principles by which the Arabs ruled, at least during the first four centuries, both religious groups were able to maintain their own beliefs and to live more or less unmolested. It was the symbiosis of the three religions and the fruitful co-existence of the different races which brought Arab rule in Spain to the height of its prosperity. History was allowed a breathing space, so to speak, as the Spanish nation was formed during this Moorish-Christian-Jewish period. The Arabs however had their fair share of political misfortune and eventually, at about the turn of the millennium, their kingdom fell. It split into innumerable so-called *taifas*, or principalities, which were constantly at war with one another.

Christian Spain

In the north of the country, on the other hand, Christian dominance was becoming firmly established. The first effective battle against the Moors was fought and won by Charlemagne who seized Catalonia. The Emperor founded the so-called Spanish frontier and placed a feudal lord as his governor in Barcelona. Two kingdoms grew up close to this frontier, Castile in the north-west and in the uplands of central Spain, and Aragón in the east, which subsequently united with Catalonia and, after its capture in 1238, with the kingdom of Valencia. Aragón became a great power in the Mediterranean and for centuries ruled over the Balearic Islands, Sardinia, Naples, Sicily and for a time even parts of Greece.

The Christian kingdoms lived for decades at peace with their Islamic neighbours, sometimes forming alliances with them and even leading them into battle against others of their Christian neighbours. Even so the aim of all Christian politics was never allowed to be forgotten, namely the expulsion from Spain of the Arab invaders. The *Reconquista*, the Reconquest, went ahead slowly but surely. In October 1479 Ferdinand, the heir to the crown of Aragón, married Isabella, the heiress to the kingdom of Castile, and as a result Spain was united into one kingdom. Their Catholic Majesties, as the royal couple were called, represent the beginning of the history of modern Spain. They strengthened the royal authority, crushed the power of the independent aristocracy, assumed authority over all the knightly orders and inaugurated a royal civil service. In addition, they brought the Reconquista to a successful conclusion when in 1492 Granada, the capital and last stronghold of the Arab kingdom, surrendered to their armies.

Rise and decline

There was yet another triumph in this fateful year of 1492. Columbus discovered America, and returning home laid a new colonial empire at the feet of Ferdinand and Isabella, who had financed his expedition. This was the beginning of a century of continuous expansion for Spain and of an incredible increase in its power and wealth. Spain became the leading nation in the Christian world. After only a hundred years, however, the decay which was to come in later centuries was already becoming evident. But it was not through exhaustion, for Spain was not lacking in daring adventurers such as Cortés and Pizarro nor in capable administrators. Although the Spanish Empire appeared at the time to be functioning economically in the most successful manner, it was nevertheless becoming saturated with the vast quantities of gold and silver which were being imported from Latin America. Money lost its value, trade began to stagnate in the mother country and agriculture suffered. It is also true that Spain lost the majority of its most skilled and industrious craftsmen and farmers. In 1609 Philip III, for reasons of state security, ordered the deportation of all the Moors who had still remained in the country following the fall of Granada.

There are no exact figures as to how many Moriscos were involved but it is known that in Aragón and Valencia alone a quarter of a million people were deported. The end of the period of tolerance had arrived. As early as 1493, the Jewish community consisting of at least 35,000 families (and according to some estimates it could have been double that figure) had been ordered to leave the country. Spain undertook this colossal purge on religious grounds and also out of concern for state security, as the east coast at that time was being plagued by Berber pirates.

The kinship that remained

The cultural inheritance from this period has remained. The language is eloquent proof of this as the number of Arabic words runs into thousands. The number of converted Moors and Jews who remained in Spain and interbred with the Christian population was probably as large as, if not larger than, the number of those who were deported. The Spanish people who have emerged from this mixture are indeed different from the rest of the European races. They have maintained a sympathetic, almost a family relationship not only towards the Jews but also towards the Moors. Consequently in the Second World War, and in spite of all the pressure from Berlin, Franco's Spain was not prepared to take any action against the Jews. On the contrary, every persecuted Jew who was able to prove that he was of Spanish descent was issued with a visa which probably saved his life. This long-established feeling of kinship is mutual. The Jews who were driven out of Spain are known as *Sephardim* and to this day speak a medieval form of Spanish even though they are scattered all over the world. This language is, with Yiddish, the second secular language of the Jewish people.

The War of the Spanish Succession

During the 15th and 16th centuries Spain was governed by the Habsburg family. Charles I of Spain was also Charles V, Emperor of Germany. Later the House of Habsburg divided into a Spanish and an Austrian branch. The last Spanish Habsburg, Charles II, died without issue in 1700 but, as a result of considerable pressure from France, he had nominated his great-nephew, Philip of Anjou, as his heir, preferring him to his Austrian nephew, the Archduke Charles. Whether from this time Spain would support France or the Habsburg empire was a political issue of the first magnitude. As a result, the War of the Spanish Succession broke out in 1701, from which France eventually emerged victorious fourteen years later. It was a costly war for Spain since the new Bourbon dynasty had to protect its recently acquired throne by renouncing territory — Gibraltar was ceded to Britain — and it was costly also for the supporters of the Austrian pretender. The old Aragonian kingdom — Aragón, Catalonia and Valencia — had sided with the Austrian claimant, and as a punishment lost its autonomous privileges, that is, its independence and its own laws. The Bourbon rulers did not succeed in giving back to Spain its former international reputation, but they did endeavour to strengthen the role of the Crown. In contrast to their Habsburg predecessors they employed the absolutist methods which they had brought with them from France, and in spite of the diversity of its traditions made Spain a centralised power.

Further decline

The Bourbon policy of dependence on their French cousins even outlasted the French Revolution and forced Spain into a catastrophic alliance with Napoleon. The family feuds of the Spanish royal house were turned to his advantage and in 1808 Napoleon persuaded the Bourbons to relinquish the throne in favour of his brother Joseph. There was an uprising by the outraged Spaniards which led to the outbreak of the Peninsular War against France.

Aided by the British, Spain freed the country from Napoleonic rule in a six-year guerrilla war, and the Bourbons withdrew to France leaving Spain devastated.

In the course of the 19th century Spain experienced three wars of succession (this time within the ruling family itself), one military uprising after another, and finally in the year 1868 the overthrow and expulsion of the ruling Queen Isabella II. The crown was offered virtually throughout Europe and it was the protest by Napoleon III against a prince from the House of Hohenzollern, giving rise to Bismarck's famous Ems Despatch, which triggered the Franco-Prussian War of 1870–71. Eventually an Italian prince offered himself for this dangerous office but Amadeo I, thwarted by the disputes within the Monarchist party, abdicated in 1872 after only two years on the throne. The Republican Party now came to the fore and a republic was proclaimed, but this was only short-lived. Parliament was dissolved and the Bourbons returned in 1875.

It was no wonder that Spain was incapable of holding on to her last colonies; in the Spanish-American War of 1898 Cuba was lost as well as Puerto Rico and the Philippines. The Spain which had been so strong in the 16th and 17th centuries now entered the 20th century as a second-class power. Fortunately, during the First World War it was able to remain neutral and this accounted for a considerable improvement in Spain's economy. In spite of this, however, in 1923 a new phase of political unrest began: the dictatorship of General Primo de Rivera, the abdication of King Alfonso XIII and the proclamation of the Second Republic, in which the differences between Left and Right were totally irreconcilable and sparked off the Spanish Civil War in 1936.

From the Civil War to the monarchy

The war lasted for three years and ended with victory for General Franco, helped by Italy and the Third Reich in Germany. The Second Republic received armaments from the Soviet Union, and volunteers came pouring in from all the western democratic states in order, as they thought, to save Spanish democracy. In the Second World War Spain managed to resist the urgent invitations from Berlin and

Rome and remained neutral. She did, however, send a division of volunteers, the 'Blue Division', to the Eastern Front.

Music festival, Valencia

Following their victory the Allied powers broke off relations with Spain, but as tension with the East grew it was received into the family of western nations again. The Franco years brought with them a considerable upward swing in Spain's economy. The boom in world commerce, tourism, low wages and an adroit economic policy all led to this expansion. After Franco's death in November 1975 a determined and complete dissolution of the former regime was carried out under the leadership of the young King Juan Carlos I. An unrestricted parliamentary democracy took its place, with a constitutional monarch at its head.

This revolutionary change took place almost without any violence or bloodshed (if one disregards the lasting terrorist threat from the Basque separatists). The entry of Spain into the European Community brought an investment boom from the middle of the eighties.

Festivals and Events

The Spaniards celebrate any occasion much more fully and lavishly than we do in Britain. Apart from the usual Catholic feast days there are others of note such as those of St James, the patron saint of Spain, on July 25th, and the Virgin of the Pillar, patron saint of all Spanish-speaking peoples and also of the Guardia Civil, on October 12th. Since the Spaniard is an individualist, however, every village and town celebrates its own festival, *fiesta* or *feria*, at a different time. The fiesta involves an extensive programme which often lasts for more than a week. During this time everybody in the whole town works for half a day only and lives it up in the evening, when the atmosphere is a mixture of the fairground and the traditional festival. In some cases this can mean that a number of bulls with blazing wax on their horns run freely through the streets with crowds of people rushing ahead of them. Alternatively, a band of 'Moors' has landed on the beach and, locked in fierce combat, attempts to drive out the 'Christians'. Every part of the country has its own speciality.

In addition to enjoyment and a lot of noise you can also experience the religious festivals, which will make a strong impression on you. The fervour and respect displayed in Holy Week processions in the south of Spain, in particular, are seldom to be found elsewhere. The figures in the processions are very heavy and are carried by *cofradías* (brotherhoods) which have been in existence for centuries and which prepare themselves throughout the year for their big moment. There are also cofradías present on the *romerías* (pilgrimages) which are popular everywhere. Here holiness and godliness combine with the fun and good humour of a picnic. Unfortunately, in places where the flood of tourists is overwhelming, the feria has become commercially exploited. However, the pleasure and enjoyment derived by the Spaniard himself from these festivals are so deep-rooted that he will always celebrate them with no inhibitions whatsoever.

Moros y Cristianos

Traditional Festivals in Eastern Spain

Els Castells: The Catalans refer to the human pyramids built by the *Xiquets* as castles. As strong as bears and as nimble as cats, these young men form their eight-man-high pyramids to the accompaniment of drums and a high-pitched oboe known as a *gralla*. A boy dances on the top of the pyramid and the greatest challenge of all is to see who can move their castle the furthest without falling in a heap. The festival is mainly to be found in Tarragona province.

Las Fallas: All over the Valencia region this traditional festival takes place on St Joseph's day, although around Alicante it is called *Hogueras/Fogueres* and is held on Midsummer Day. The festival is reputed to have its origins in the spring holiday of the Carpenters' Guild which was celebrated on the day of their patron saint, Joseph. The carpenters ritually burned the enormous wooden candlesticks which had provided light for them in their gloomy workshops during the winter months. Originally the candlesticks were decorated with the accumulation of the year's wood shavings, using glue and paint. The massive effigies of the Fallas of today no longer bear much resemblance to those of the past. Every district of the town in Valencia has its own *Falleros*, members of a committee who work together on these enormous groups of allegorical figures. They are constructed for effect rather than artistic merit and the largest can be as high as a five- or six-storey building. They do not follow any particular traditional pattern but attempt instead to express contemporary ideas. On March 19th, the highlight of the festival is reached when the *Cremá* or burning takes place. The Fallas, which have cost a small fortune to make, are set on fire and burned to the rumble of drums. This is, of course, the most exciting part of the Fallas and usually takes place on one of the small squares of the town. The figures, as high as the surrounding houses, must be so constructed that they do not topple over to one side. Firemen spray the façades of the houses to prevent them catching fire. There are plenty of fireworks, too, during this *nit del foc* – night of fire.

Encierro and toro embolado: The *encierro* is all about bulls, not in the arena but running free through the streets with a crowd of people ahead of them. On a given signal the young bulls are released and begin to run close behind the village youths. One variation of the encierro is the *toro embolado*, the 'bull with blobs of wax on its horns'. It is in principle quite similar, except that the bull is released after midnight and both horns are mounted with blazing blobs of wax. As a tourist, it is better to limit yourself to the role of spectator!

Moros y Cristianos: This is another festival which takes place mainly in the Valencia region. 'Moors and Christians' fight it out in spectacular mock versions of the battles between the Arabs and the Spaniards. The event is usually dedicated to the local patron saint, to whose help is attributed the taking of the town by the Christians. Everyone in the town takes part, all in medieval costume, and the whole performance — invasion, negotiations, and the taking of prisoners — can last for days on end. The most renowned are the Moros y Cristianos of Alcoy and Villajoyosa.

The bullfight is a national pastime in Spain but it does not take place all the year round. *Corridas de toros* or simply toros are held only during a particular season, which begins at different times of the year according to the town or city and lasts for several weeks. From February to October, a corrida will always be taking place somewhere in Spain.

Do not expect to see a 'show', but get into the right frame of mind for an aesthetic performance of art and courage, whose subject is quite simply life and death. The corrida is, of course, unique and any comparison with other forms of sport or display is quite impossible. As a tourist it is important therefore to get some information about the bullfight from an *aficionado*, an expert on the subject. Preferably avoid corridas which are held in tourist towns, as the right atmosphere does not come through if the public seats are occupied by foreigners alone. The seats are divided into different price ranges according to their proximity to the arena, and into 'shady', 'sunny', or 'sunny and shady' positions (*sombra, sol,* and *sol y sombra*). You are advised to take the shady side as you will then be more likely to sit amongst the Spanish aficionados than among other holidaymakers.

The bullfight

It is important to be aware of the fact that in a bullfight the bull (*toro*) and the bullfighter (*torero*) are equal in the eyes of the aficionados. There is an expectancy that both will provide a fight which unfolds with all the drama of a Classical tragedy. In order to do honour to the splendour of the occasion, it must be performed with style and as perfectly as possible. Anything else would be considered a degradation of the event and of the ceremony. The qualities required of a bullfighter are courage, elegance, skill and a regard for the bull as a worthy opponent. The bull is expected to be as noble as the bullfighter, as nobody wishes to see the slaughter of a cowardly animal in the arena. If the bull is a good one, then he will fight with all the natural courage and

inborn tenacity of a Spanish fighting bull, a *toro bravo*. For that reason, any thoughts of cruelty to animals should be forgotten. A variation is the *rejoneo* or mounted bullfight. It takes place only rarely and is older than the fight on foot. An opportunity to see the *rejoneador* and his horse in action should not be missed. The horses are brilliantly trained and in moments of danger perform dance steps and figures equal to those of the Spanish riding school in Vienna.

Flamenco: Next to the bullfight the flamenco, song and dance, is the best-known Spanish cultural phenomenon. At the same time, it is certainly not common throughout Spain but is restricted to Andalusia where it is the heart and soul of folk music. In fact it is peculiar to only two of the regions covered in this volume, namely Murcia and Almería.

Flamenco expresses the Spanish temperament

In layman's terms one can identify two distinct types of flamenco, the one that is danced and the one that is only sung. Both have their origins in the very distant past, but experts see in flamenco traces of Byzantine choral music, the feeling of gipsy music and a great deal of Arab influence. The danced flamenco in both the tragic and cheerful variants is a breathtaking performance. The movements of the dancer are very oriental, the feet and above all the hands playing a major role. If men dance with women then they do so only with rather restrained, peremptory movements. It is thus that the passions are expressed. More demanding, however, are the *cante jondo* and the *soleá* which are not danced. Instead the singer and the guitarist sit alone. Verses are often made up on the spur of the moment and are sung in highly polished, tragic, almost sobbing semitones. The performance reflects the degree to which Christian and Moorish cultures have intertwined in the peninsula.

✂ Food and Drink

Strictly speaking, Spanish cuisine is scarcely known at all abroad. Just how much do we know about it? *Paella*, the rice dish, will sometimes come to mind and perhaps even *gazpacho*, the delicious cold soup from Andalusia. But what else?

More so than other European cuisines, that of Spain is characterised by regional specialities, some of which are obtainable all over the country and some of which can be found only in their place of origin. Most cooking is done with olive oil. Butter was practically unknown until about 20 years ago and it tends to be rather rancid even when used today!

Tapas

These are traditionally Spanish. Piled high on the counters of every bar you will find these titbits which should be sampled with a glass of wine, sherry or beer. Tiny fish, grilled, baked or marinated, chunks of meat prepared with different sauces, squid, shrimps, mussels, mayonnaise salads, tortillas, ham and cheese are all to be found. Particularly tasty is *jamón serrano*, a ham which is dried in the open air, or *jabugo* and the mature *manchego,* cheeses made from a blend of cow's and sheep's milk.

Soups

Soups do not play a very large part in Spanish cuisine. The exception, of course, is *gazpacho*, an Andalusian chilled, hot-weather soup. It is made from olive oil, tomatoes, cucumbers, sweet peppers, onions, garlic and bread. Croutons and other diced accompaniments are served as a garnish. It is a masterpiece in its inspired simplicity.

Seafood and fish

Fish is eaten and enjoyed throughout the country. There is the fish soup *sopa de pescado (suc de peix)* which is related to the French bouillabaisse, and *mejillones al vino blanco*, sea mussels served in white wine. Shellfish are particularly popular although not always good value for money. Lobsters (*langostas* or the smaller *langostinos*), enormous shrimps known as *carabineros* because their deep red colour is reminiscent of the uniforms once worn by Customs officials, and the Mediterranean shrimps (*gambas*) which are obtainable everywhere are all worth trying.

The larger shellfish are grilled with salt (*a la plancha*) or boiled and served with a mayonnaise sauce. The smaller varieties are usually prepared *al ajillo*, in oil with garlic and spices. Before prejudging it why not try squid (*calamares*) which is very popular in Spain. It is delicious fried in batter (*fritos*) or cooked in its own juices (*en su tinta*). Fish is good grilled (*a la plancha*) or cooked in oil (*frito*), or even casseroled. The most popular types of fish are sole (*lenguado*), tuna (*bonito*), halibut (*mero*), haddock (*merluza*) and tender filleted swordfish (*pez de espada*) which is grilled in steak-sized portions. A delicacy from Valencia is the eel (*all i pebre*), cooked as goujons in a paprika and garlic sauce. Highly rated is the young eel (*angula*) which is simmered in oil and garlic. Sometimes the fish is offered *a la sal*, baked in a block of salt which is opened in front of the guest. This method of cooking preserves the natural juices of the fish particularly well. Sardines (*sardinas*) are always very good, as are *chanquetes* which are even smaller than sardines.

Seafood

Paella

There are countless varieties of this main-course dish, each varying according to region and mood. Basically the recipe is simply rice, saffron and anything else you like to add. Sometimes it is just made with fish, sometimes with meat such as poultry, pork, rabbit or game, and sometimes with both. The name stems from the large, flat pan in which the delicacy is prepared. Paella must always be freshly made; in good restaurants you should expect to wait for at least half an hour, and it should if possible be cooked over an orangewood fire.

Valencia offers other related rice specialities, one of the best being *arroz a banda*, a type of risotto. The rice is cooked in water in which fish with the most piquant flavour has previously been cooked. It sounds simple but it is in fact very good. In Murcia, a similar dish is known as *arroz caldero*.

Arroz al forn, rice baked in the oven, is very popular too. Another variation of paella is found in Gandía, the *fideuá*, where noodles take the place of rice. This is prepared with seafood or *a banda*.

Tortilla

This is a typical Spanish dish. In its traditional form it is known as *tortilla de patatas* or *española* and it is made into an omelette filled with fried diced potatoes, onions and vegetables. It may be eaten cold or hot and varied in any way whatsoever. A typical *tapa* is a *pincho de tortilla*.

Meat

Beef is not a Spanish speciality and is only served satisfactorily in the better restaurants. Chicken (*pollo*), however, is always good. Particularly recommended are roast lamb (*cordero asado*) and sucking pig (*cochinillo*). Ordinary roast pork is always excellent too.

Dessert

In spite of the efforts made by the Spaniards to popularise the sweet pastries which were inherited from the Moors, they are unfortunately not often found in restaurants. Instead you must go to a *confitería*, a confectioner's. You can always get *flan*, a type of creme caramel, in a restaurant, or the similar but incomparably better *tocina de cielo*, 'bacon from heaven'! Why not try *manzanas asadas*, baked apples, or *peras en vino*, pears in wine, which are also very good. If you go to Valencia do not forget to try their oranges and, in season, some fresh figs (*higos*). Then there are *churros*, a kind of fritter, deep fried, and delicious with a drink of hot chocolate.

Gazpacho – the refreshing summer soup from Andalusia. For four people.

3 cucumbers, 1 large white onion, 6 large ripe tomatoes, 4 red sweet peppers, 2 cloves of garlic, ½ teaspoonful of vinegar, 1 cup of olive oil, salt, ½ teaspoonful of sugar, 3 slices of white bread.

Peel the cucumbers and slice finely, removing any large seeds. Cut the tomatoes into quarters and lightly coat in oil. Peel the onion and chop coarsely. Halve the pepper, remove the seeds and cut into thin strips. Prepare the cloves of garlic by cutting into small pieces and crushing in a china or wooden mortar. Cut the bread into small cubes. Sieve the tomatoes or put them into a blender. Put the liquid into a mixer and add the onion, cucumber, garlic, peppers, olive oil, sugar and bread. Mix. Add some ice to thin it down and to cool the soup. Season with salt and pepper. Serve the soup ice-cold. Chopped cucumber, tomatoes, peppers, hard boiled eggs, onions and croutons can be added as garnish.

Drink

Lunch always finishes with a good coffee, either black (*café solo*) or with a drop of milk (*café cortado*). With this a glass of excellent Spanish cognac (*coñac*) can be taken. (Officially this must be called 'brandy' because of trademark regulations.) The cheap brands *Fundador, Centenario* and *103* are very good. If you would like to try the very best, then have a *Cardenal Mendoza, Lepanto* or *Carlos I*. The classic liqueur is *anis*, sweet or dry (*dulce* or *seco*); the best brands are *Chinchón* or *Cadenas*. Known throughout Europe and always very popular is sherry (*jerez*); the following types can be recommended. *Fino* or *seco*, dry, light and sharp and with a slight almond flavour, should be chilled before drinking; good brands are *La Ina, Tío Pepe* and *Tío Mateo*. *Oloroso* is full-bodied, dark and either dry or sweet, the best brands being *Río Viejo* which is dry and *Oloroso Dulce* which is sweet. *Dulce* is a dark sweet dessert wine and a good brand is *Pedro Ximénez*.

Similar but lighter than the dry sherries are the *Montilla* and *Moriles* wines from Córdoba province (brand: *Alvear C.B.*), whilst the sweet *Málaga* wine compares very favourably with the Dulce.

The table wines of Spain are usually first class, although the white wines have their limitations. Red wines come chiefly from the *Rioja* region, the lighter white wines from *Valdepeñas*. Catalonia and Valencia also have well known wine-producing regions. Good value are the house wines (*vino de la casa*) which are stocked in every bar. In addition mineral water can be ordered, sparkling or still (*agua mineral con gas* or *sin gas*), which can be mixed with the wine. Very popular among tourists is *sangría*, a cold refreshing drink made from wine, lemonade, orange and lemon juice, pieces of fruit and a drop of cognac.

The Catalan champagne (*champán* or *vino de cava*) is also very good. The *Freixenet* or *Codorniú* brands are recommended.

Shopping in the Rambla San Carlos, Tarragona

Shopping

Spain has much to offer the visitor from abroad.

Craftwork of all types is to be found in most places. Almost every village has one market day during the week. You should enquire when this *mercado* or *mercadillo* is held. In addition to lots of trinkets you will always find something worth taking home. It is especially worth while visiting the towns and villages which specialise in a particular product. You are then able to buy direct from the manufacturer and have a very wide range to choose from. Further information will be found under the individual place names. In the larger towns there are not only souvenir shops catering for tourists but also specialist shops where you can find the particular carpet, plate or lamp you are looking for. The relevant departments in the large stores also might well have exactly what you want.

Pottery from Spain is very popular throughout Europe. The different 'schools' or production centres of Spanish *cerámica* or *alfarería* are scattered all over the country. The most important are listed below. *Manises*, near Valencia, specialises in refined, brightly painted pieces and sometimes very fine filigree work. White pottery is also particularly attractive; it is of such superior quality that it is almost equal to porcelain. Pottery from *Teruel* is rustic in style with attractive Moorish and medieval designs in black, green and white. *Granada* specialises in bird and flower motifs in blue-white and blue-green. *Toledo (Puente del Arzobispo, Talavera)*, on the other hand, produces very colourful work but preference is shown for charming animal and hunting scenes in green, white and light brown. Glazed pottery for everyday use in the kitchen and in the house, such as oil jars or heat-proof dishes, is also to be found there. This type of ware is usually only partly glazed, in brown or green.

Baskets and raffia work (*mimbre* and *esparto*) are made in many parts of Valencia, Alicante and Murcia. Anything and everything made from cane and raffia can be found here. Particularly hardwearing and decorative are the plain or multi-coloured esparto carpets. Everything you see here will be found in the large furniture shops in the UK but at very much higher prices. It might even be worth while buying a large item and having it exported. The manager of the shop will be only too willing to arrange it for you.

Embroidery (*bordados*) on linen or cotton, especially table linen, is produced in Toledo but is obtainable everywhere.

Leather (*cuero*): Spain, like Italy, is world-famous for its leatherware. Spanish shoes (*zapatos*), which come mainly from Alicante, are very good value. The price, quality and variety of handbags (*bolsos de mano*) compare favourably with those in the UK. Leather jackets and coats (*chaquetas, abrigos de piel*) are very popular and cheap to buy.

Metalwork has an age-old tradition. Brass (*metal amarillo, latón*), copper (*cobre*) and bronze (*bronce*) goods are produced everywhere. There is a very good mixture of old patterns and modern designs, and you can find everything from teapots to lamps in these materials. Spanish tin (*estaño*) which comes from the region of Segovia in Castile is of particularly good quality and is cheap. Articles from Granada made from tin-plate (*hojalata*) are a speciality of Moorish origin. These are mainly in the form of lamps and chandeliers, some of which have coloured glass. For the amateur artist the tin lamps are a special delight, as it is customary to buy them unpainted and to decorate them at home.

Antiques (*antigüedades*) can be found in the antique shops (*anticuarios*) or in the flea-market (*rastro, rastrillo*), but as in the rest of Europe the sources of antiques have almost dried up. Nevertheless, it is still possible to discover articles, particularly curios from the last hundred years, which in this country would fetch collectors' prices.

Fashion and clothing: In addition to the smart boutiques found in the holiday resorts and large towns, there are also big department stores in the provincial capitals (*El Corte Inglés, Galerías Preciados*) which hold their summer sales (*rebajas*) in August, timed just right to suit the tourist. In perfumes, cosmetics, accessories and fashion jewellery Spanish firms have much to offer. Try *Puig, Elio Bernhayer, Loewe* or *Myrurgia*.

Food and drink: Olive oil (*aceite de oliva*) is inexpensive in Spain and has a better flavour than the oil sold in Britain. Brands such as *Carbonell, Koipe* or *Elosua* are particularly good.

Sherry, cognac, aniseed liqueur and wine are all considerably cheaper than in this country. Turrón, the Spanish nougat (see *Jijona*, page 71), makes a delicious treat for friends at home.

Hints for your holiday

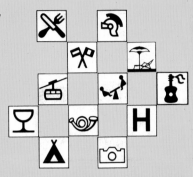

When in Spain...

It goes without saying that a friendly manner and respect for the customs of their country will be appreciated by your Spanish hosts. Here are just a few tips to remember. Make the effort to learn a few words of Spanish; it will stand you in very good stead. *Por favor* (please) and *gracias* (thank you), *holá* (hello) and *hasta luego* (until the next time) are all words which people everywhere like to hear. Swimwear belongs on the beach. In towns, as you will find everywhere along the Mediterranean coast, men in shorts and lightly clad women are quite out of place. In churches this sort of attire is considered completely improper.

Whenever you meet Spaniards always try to return their hospitality. This does not mean just saying a formal 'please' or 'thank you'. Be generous – offer them a cigarette or maybe a beer and perhaps your company. The Spanish people hate meanness. Although Spaniards enjoy a drink, drunkards are seldom seen. Indeed, although they can often drink quite a lot they have little sympathy for real drunkenness. When it comes to holiday romances, remember that Spanish youths like the Italians are constantly on the look-out for 'blonde prey'. Englishmen however be warned — there is a taboo on Spaniards' wives, so beware the proverbial Spanish jealousy! The same applies to the Spaniard's pride and you should therefore guard your tongue when talking to local people about Spain. Amongst themselves they complain all day long about the state of the country, but they would never dream of speaking in the same terms to a foreigner.

If you comply with these simple guidelines, then you will be looked upon as a friend by the Spanish people, and will be welcomed as a guest rather than tolerated as a customer.

Tamarit castle on the Costa Dorada

Where to go and what to see

Costa Dorada

The stretch of country covered by this book under the heading of the 'Golden Coast' is sandwiched between Tarragona and the vast, isolated lowlands of the Ebro delta. Every type of attraction a tourist could wish for lies within this area. The Costa Dorada (Costa Daurada) belongs to the province of Tarragona which in turn forms part of the autonomous region of Catalonia (*Cataluña, Catalunya*). In addition to Spanish you will also hear the rather nasal sounds of Catalan.

The main route to be followed is the N-340 coastal road from north to south, with occasional trips into the hinterland. For any lengthy stages of the route you are strongly advised to use the A-7 toll motorway, which lies parallel to the N-340 and is quite often not so busy. In the following pages you will find the appropriate motorway exit numbers (e.g. AA-7) given after the names of places on the route.

Tarragona Pop. 140,000

This is the capital of the province of the same name and is the see of one of the oldest bishoprics in Spain. It lies on a hill which slopes down gradually to the sea. The town's most prosperous periods were under the Romans and in the early Middle Ages, when the population was very much greater than it is today. The monuments which remain from those days are really splendid and make a visit to Tarragona memorable. As a holiday resort, however, the town cannot be recommended as the beaches have become polluted by the waste from the nearby refineries. It is better to stay at

Roman arch near Tarragona

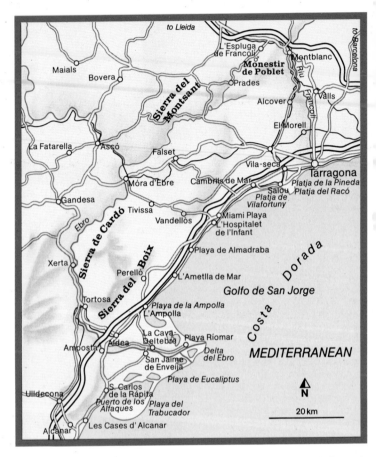

one of the seaside resorts such as Salou or Cambrils.

It is not known who actually founded Tarragona. Local legend attributes the first colonisation to Tubal, the grandson of Noah! It is certain that when they captured Tarragona in the year 218 B.C. the Romans found a large town surrounded by 'cyclopean' walls. Tarraco, as the Romans called it, owed its swift advance to the Scipios. The two Scipios, grandfather and grandson, both famous Roman generals, built up in Tarragona one of the most important strongholds of the Roman legions in Hispania. About fifty years later, Tarraco became the capital of the Roman province of *Hispania Citerior*, which was later called simply *Tarraconensis*. Christianity came early to Tarragona. In fact, it is quite probable that the Apostle Paul preached there. This early Christian connection led to the archbishops of Tarragona claiming the primacy among the Spanish bishops, but the attempt was unsuccessful.

The town never again reached such an important position as it did during the Roman occupation. Moorish rule lasted from A.D. 714 until the turn of the century. During the following centuries, Tarragona underwent several changes of ownership, until it finally came under Christian domination in the year A.D. 1220. In the Middle Ages Tarragona, as a port and trading centre, profited from the wealth of the kingdom of Aragón but was only of moderate importance. Ecclesiastical life, however, flourished and the cathedral, one of the most splendid examples of Gothic architecture in Spain, testifies to this. It is only in recent decades since important industrial undertakings have become established in the area that Tarragona has experienced an upswing in its fortunes.

The Upper Town

The Upper Town, a network of tiny narrow alleyways, is bordered partly by the old city wall at the Passeig Arqueológic on one side, and by the Rambla Vella and the Passeig Sant Antoni on the other. A little way to the south-east of the Rambla Vella you come to the central hub of Tarragona, the Rambla Nova. This avenue ends at the *Balcó del Mediterrani* (the Mediterranean Balcony), which provides a splendid view over the Roman amphitheatre. The statue of the medieval knight represents Roger de Lauria, one of the admirals of Aragón. It is just a step or two from the Balcó to the Calle San Hermenegildo which leads from the Rambla Vella to the Plaça del Rei.

The Palau de August

The Emperor Augustus, who spent the years A.D. 25 to 27 in Tarragona, gave his name to this austere fortified stone building which towers over the surrounding area. It is also referred to as

the *Palau del Rei* (the King's Palace), probably after the Aragón monarchs who converted part of this Roman stronghold into a residence. However, it might also be a reference to the Visigothic rebel king Hermenegild, who rose up against his father, Leovigild, because the latter followed the teachings of the Arian Heresy, a form of Christianity adopted by the Vandals. After subjecting his son to long periods of torture, Leovigild eventually had him beheaded in front of the fortress on Easter Saturday in the year 585.

The building today forms part of the *Museu Arqueológico* which provides a very clear picture of the life and art of Roman Tarraco. In one of the rooms you can see part of the pre-Roman 'cyclopean' wall, so called because the massive blocks of stone were joined together without any form of mortar, almost as though a mythological giant had been at work.

In addition, parts of several Roman temples in Tarraco have been assembled here and are on display, together with busts of its rulers. Also to be seen are some magnificent floor mosaics, depicting marine life and a head of Medusa. There is also a remarkable ivory doll with movable limbs. (Open: Summer 10 a.m.–1 p.m. and 4.30–8 p.m. Winter 10 a.m.–1.30 p.m. and 4–7 p.m. Closed Sunday afternoon and Monday.)

The cathedral

The *Catedral* or *Seu* is reached by making your way north through the little medieval streets. Work was begun on the cathedral following the first Christian conquest of the city at the beginning of the 12th c. It was started in the Romanesque style as a fortified church and was considerably extended and modified on several occasions subsequently. Particularly attractive are the many forms of Gothic architecture which are represented here. The main

Tarragona Cathedral cloisters

decorated with a 13th c. Romanesque marble relief which also depicts scenes from the martyrdom of the beloved saint.

The *Capilla Santa María de los Sastres,* to the left of the high altar, is dedicated to St Mary, the patron saint of tailors. This five-sided chapel was built at the beginning of the 14th c. by English master builders and is, with its typical Minstrels' Gallery, a rare example of English Gothic architecture in its purest form. To the right of the high altar is the marble sarcophagus of Prince Juan of Aragón who, after 33 years as Archbishop of Tarragona, died in the year 1334. His tomb is the work of an anonymous, possibly Italian, sculptor.

The group of figures in the *Santo Sepulcro* chapel near the chancel depicts the burial of Christ. The marble figure of Christ lies in a Roman sarcophagus of the 4th c. and is surrounded by 15th c. painted stone figures. If you go through the magnificent Romanesque doorway to the left of the high altar, you come to the *claustro* (cloisters). Above the exceptionally well preserved doorway are representations of Christ and the symbols of the Evangelists. Matthew appears as a winged man, Mark as a winged lion, Luke as a winged bull and John as an eagle. The cloisters were built in the transitional period between Romanesque and Gothic, and elements of both styles are represented. 211 marble capitals are richly decorated with all kinds of themes, both religious and secular. Leaving the cloisters you come to the *Museu Diocesá,* where the cathedral's treasures are on display. In addition to a comprehensive collection of Gothic altar panels by Catalan artists — look especially at St Michael's altar by Bernat Martorell and the 15th c. Lady altar by Lluís Borrassá — there is a particularly valuable collection of Flemish tapestries of the 15th to 17th c., which in some cases are based on sketches by Rubens and Jordaens.

façade is dominated by its massive doorway. The statue of the Madonna on the column which divides the entrance is the work of the Norman master craftsman Bartolomé (late 13th c.), as are the apostles to the right and left of the doorway. Above the right-hand doorway can be seen a beautifully decorated 3rd c. sarcophagus let into the wall.

The interior of the cathedral, which consists of three aisles, is certainly Gothic in style but without the usual lofty spaciousness. Here you are reminded of the cathedral's original plan, that of a fortified church, solid and compact. The two side aisles are flanked by splendid original chapels.

The famous high altar is in the *Capilla Mayor.* It was created between 1426 and 1433 by the Catalan sculptor Pere Johan. Scenes from the life and martyrdom of St Thecla, the patron saint of Tarragona, are colourfully painted on alabaster and marble. The main figures on the altar are the Madonna, St Thecla and the Apostle Paul, who was indirectly responsible for St Thecla's suffering as it was he who had converted her to Christianity. The front of the altar is

Biblical and allegorical scenes are depicted on the 54 tapestries. (Cathedral, cloisters and museum are open from 10 a.m.–12.30 p.m. and from 4–7 p.m., except on Sunday mornings.)

The Old Town

If you take a leisurely stroll through the alleyways of the Old Town you will be transported back to the Middle Ages. You will also find several interesting Roman arches on the way. Hebrew inscriptions appear on the window ledge of a house in the Carrer Escribanies Vellas. Houses of the nobility stand in the *Carrer Cavallers* (Gentlemen's Street). A civic museum, *Casa-Museu de Castellarnau*, was opened in one of these mansions which belonged formerly to the Castellarnau family. This house is worth a visit not only to view its collection of coins and ceramics but also because of its furnishings and architecture. The beautiful vaulted ceilings of the lower rooms are supported by Roman arches which came originally from the circus. These and the superb inner courtyard with its Gothic staircase were both well known to the Emperor Charles V when he resided here in 1542. The upper ·reception rooms contain furniture which dates from the 17th–19th c. Make sure you see the 18th c. neo-Classical ceiling frescos by the Provençal artist Josep Bernat Flaugier. (Open: 10 a.m.–1 p.m. and 4–7 p.m. daily except Monday and Sunday afternoons.)

Roman remains

These can be found everywhere. On the north side of the cathedral a Roman wall surrounds the Old Town. An idyllic promenade lined by shady trees runs between the wall and a group of fortified buildings of later date. This avenue, which is open to the public from 9 a.m. to 8 p.m. except Sunday afternoons and Mondays, is known as the *Passeig Arqueológic*.

Olive trees in typical Costa Dorada landscape, Pinell de Bray, Tarragona

The Roman wall, which is very well preserved, is about 1 km in length. Of considerable interest is the pre-Roman 'cyclopean' lower section some 2 or 3 metres in height and containing several small doorways. The fortifications on the

Puente del Diablo — Roman aqueduct outside Tarragona

Amphitheatre, Tarragona

other side of the Passeig probably date back to the Middle Ages. The cannons which stand there, however, date from the War of the Spanish Succession (1701–14) during which Tarragona, under the French, was badly damaged. A statue of the Emperor Augustus stands close to the *Torre de l'Arquebisbe*. This was presented to the town by the Italians to celebrate the 2000th anniversary of his birth. After you have enjoyed the wonderful view over the countryside and the sea from the tower, you should continue your tour of the town centre. If you go via the Passeig Torroja you will come to the Passeig Sant Antoni which takes you along the southern part of the city wall to the Plaça del Rei. This stretch of the wall with its fine St Anthony's Gate and Cross was incorporated into the houses which were later built there. Everywhere you will see beautiful latticed windows.

At the intersection close to the Plaça del Rei where the Rambla Vella and the Via Augusta cross, the winding Passeig del Miracle leads to the remains of the *amfiteatre* (amphitheatre). Within the elliptical form of the ancient building you can see the ground plan of a Visigothic basilica built in honour of St Fructuosus who, together with his deacons, was

burnt to death on this site in the year A.D. 257.

The remains of the Roman *forum* or market place can be found in the Carrer de Lleida behind the main post office (correos) in the New Town. Pillars and arches from what was in the 2nd c. A.D. one of the most important sites in the city, comprising law courts, temples and shops, still remain standing in the square courtyard. (Open: 10 a.m.– 1 p.m. and 4–7 p.m. Closed Sunday afternoon and Monday.) To the west of the forum via the Avinguda Ramón y Cajal you will come to the *Necrópolis* (City of the Dead) on the banks of the Francolí River. The Early Christian Museum (*Museu Paleocristiá*) can also be found there. In 1926, when a tobacco factory was being built, a Christian burial ground was discovered containing over 2000 graves from the 3rd to 5th c. The tombs and mosaics are displayed in the museum which was erected on the actual site of the discovery. (Opening times as above.)

Sol Ric, Via Augusta 227, with gardens close to the sea; *C'al Brut*, San Pedro 14; *La Puda*, Muelle de Pescadores; *Meson del Mar*, Playa Largo, Ctra. de Barcelona.

Oficina Municipal de Turismo, Carrer Mayor 39; tel.(977) 23 89 22. *Oficina de Turisme*, Fortuny 4; tel.(977) 23 34 15.

Excursions

Drive along the coastal road to *Tamarit* castle (8 km to the north of Tarragona) or alternatively head towards Lleida on the N-240 and go through Valls and the Coll de l'Illa pass to Montblanc (36 km). At the pass you will find a hotel restaurant which serves good food and from where there is a fine view. Leaving Montblanc, branch off to the left and go via L'Espluga de Francolí to the monastery of Poblet (a further 7 km).

Valls

The best times to see the human pyramids (*castells*) created by the *Xiquets* of Valls are June 24th (*Festes de Sant Joan*) and the first Sunday after October 21st (*Fira de Santa Úrsula*).

 Oficina de Informació Municipal; tel. (977) 60 10 50.

Montblanc

This town was founded in A.D. 1162 by Alfonso the Chaste of Aragón and raised to a duchy of the Aragón monarchy in the 14th c. by Martin the Humane. In later years, however, Montblanc sank into complete insignificance, which perhaps explains why the medieval structure of the town has remained unchanged. The 1½-km-long town wall with its two gates and 28 towers has been almost perfectly preserved.

Enter the town by the tower gate, *Torre Portal de Bové*, and bear left and then right into the Carrer del Corts. On the left you will see the Romanesque church of *San Miguel* where the Catalan parliament, the Corts, sat on four occasions. Supported by Gothic interior arches is a fine painted wooden ceiling. Standing in the same square is the compact *Palau del Castellà*, the palace of the governor who was the representative of the king in the town. If you now follow the main road, Carrer Major, to the right and then turn left, you will come to the attractive main square, the *Plaza Mayor*. On the left there is a 14th–16th c. mansion, *Casal dels Desclerques*, with an elegant doorway, and on the right is the town hall, *Casa de la Vila*. Built in the 13th c. in the Gothic style, it has a Baroque doorway, balcony and gallery. Weights and measures were checked by officials on market day beneath the Gothic arcade with its pointed arches. Diagonally across from

Town wall, Montblanc

the town hall is the principal fountain, *Font Mayor*, which dates from 1804 and is adorned with a huge Spanish crest. Now turn back and take the first street on the left. You are now at the foot of the hill, which is completely surrounded by the wall, and which is known as the *Plá de Santa Bárbara*, or the 'White Hill'; hence the name of the town. The imposing parish church of *Santa María la Mayor* stands on the hillside. Construction work was begun on the church in 1352, by the (probably English) master builder Reynard des Fonoll, who also carried out work on Tarragona Cathedral. Have a look at the 17th c. Baroque doorway which is in stark contrast to the pure Gothic style of the rest of the building. Inside there is a stone altar dedicated to Saints Bernard and Barnabas, as well as a fine 17th c. organ.

 Oficina Municipal de Turisme (in the Town Hall), Plaza Mayor 1; tel.(977) 86 00 09.

Poblet

Set in rolling countryside, the monastery of Poblet can be seen from far away. The lovingly restored building is one of the centres of Catalan cultural and ecclesiastical life. The atmosphere of

Santa María, Montblanc

Interior of Santa María

the place — contemplative and yet also stimulating — will almost certainly make you wish to stay here for several days. The Santa María monastery was founded in 1151 by Duke Ramon Berenguer IV of Barcelona, in gratitude for a successful campaign against the Moors in the surrounding highlands. Cistercian monks, whose order had not at that time been long established, were sent for from the French monastery at Fontfroide. By rendering cultivable the desolate surrounding land they made it possible for settlement to continue in the future. Ramon's marriage to Petronilla, heiress to the kingdom of Aragón, united the two realms. His descendants made Poblet their favourite monastery, choosing to be buried there, building a palace in its grounds and providing huge sums of money over the centuries for its endowment. In 1835, however, monastic life in Poblet came to a sudden halt. When church property was confiscated by the liberal government in Madrid the monks were forced to flee. The buildings were plundered and soon fell into decay. The monastery remained in this condition for almost a hundred years, until in 1930 a society of 'Friends of the Monastery' was formed. At the heart of the project was a gifted Catalan,

Eduardo Toda i Güell, whose castle of Escornalbou near Cambrils (see page 31) you may like to visit. The restoration of large parts of the ruined buildings enabled the Cistercians to return in 1940, forming a community which is still thriving today. The monastery is also a cultural centre of Catalonia; especially well known is its publishing house, which specialises in Catalan historical research.

Descriptions of the monastic buildings are not given here as only guided tours are permitted. It can be said, however, that thanks to the excellent restoration work that has been undertaken here, you will seldom find such a complete picture of medieval monastic life.

Salou Pop. 10,000; AA-36

This is the largest seaside resort on the Costa Dorada. Situated on the cape of the same name, it was formerly the coastal district of Vila Seca which lies further inland. It has long since outstripped Vila Seca, however, and has acquired the rather grand nickname of *Playa de Europa* — not without good reason, though, as Salou exists purely for tourists and in the winter months is extremely quiet. The huge complex is in quite good taste, if somewhat artificial-looking. Wide avenues of palm trees border the main beach, ending by an illuminated fountain. Tall apartment blocks are everywhere but luckily they are not crowded too closely together. Relatively speaking the number of hotels is quite small, as the majority of tourists seem to prefer holiday flats.

 To the west of the rocky cape, the large *Playas del Poniente* are situated on either side of the marina. In a rocky setting, but cleaner and not so busy, are the small *Playa dels Capellans* and *Playa Larga*. Small sandy inlets lie at the foot of the headland, which is covered with pine woods. To the east, 3 km from the town, is the long *Playa de la Pineda*. All the beaches mentioned consist of fine sand.

 Casa Solé, Ctra. Salou-Cambrils.

 Pizzeria Piazza Fontana, c. Saragossa; *Casa Font*, c. Colom.

 Saint Germain, Plaza Provincia; *Caballo Blanco*, c. Bruselas; *Flashback*, Plaza Europa.

Barlovento, Passeig Miramar (with live music); *Claqué*, Ctra. Salou-Cambrils; *Jardin de las Delicias*, c. Reus.

Oficina Municipal de Turisme, Esplanada del Port; tel. (977) 38 02 33.

Cambrils AA-37

The attractive little harbour and picturesque town centre of Cambrils owe their charm to the fact that they are quite unspoilt. In this delightful and rather rustic atmosphere you feel (as you cannot in Salou) that you are in touch with the real Spain.

A fine long sandy bay extends eastwards from the harbour

Salou

towards Salou; there are small bays with breakwaters to the west.

  Pedalos.

 Piscina Municipal, Cambrils-Bahía.

 Deportes Mariné, Passeig La Salle.

 Centro de Equitación, Vilafortuny.

 On the road to Salou.

 Pista Municipal, Cambrils-Bahía.

Mas Gallau, Ctra. Barcelona; *Casa Gallau*, c. Pescadores 25 (speciality: fish dishes); *Shanghai* (Chinese).

Centre d'Iniciatives i Turisme, Plaça Creu de la Missió 1; tel. (977) 36 11 59.

To the *Parque Samá* botanical gardens (5 km) and to the romantic castle of *San Miguel de Escornalbou* (20 km).

 South of Cambrils is camping land with one campsite after another.

In general only campers are allowed access to the beach, but in some places there is also public access. Once on the seashore, however, you can move around quite freely as there are no private beaches in Spain.

Miami Playa AA-38

Hopes are raised when you hear the name of this seaside resort, but unfortunately these are not fulfilled. The whole area consists of a few dilapidated apartment blocks and pensioners' houses. There is no real town centre.

 A fairly large sandy beach, *Playa de Cristal*, close to the development of the same name. Various little sandy bays in Miami Playa itself.

 Pedalos.

 Casablanca, Playa de Cristal development.

The shoreline changes between Miami Playa and the Ebro delta. The sandy beach gives way to rocks, and only small inlets which are difficult to get to are suitable for bathing.

On the other hand, the towns are quieter — they are real little fishing ports — and there are fewer tourists.

L'Hospitalet de l'Infant AA-38

This township has a small harbour for fishing- and pleasure-boats. In the southernmost part there is a beautiful long sandy beach, but only a short distance away the cooling towers of the Vandellós Nuclear Power Station dominate the rocky landscape. Almost in the shadow of these towers you can turn left to the tiny sandy inlet of *Playa de Almadraba*. Fringed only by a few bungalows, it is favoured by the French engineers who work at the power station.

   La Almadraba.

L'Ametlla de Mar AA-39

This is a really genuine little fishing village clinging to the side of a steep slope. Close to the harbour are cafés where you can sit outside and watch the fishing fleet returning home at about 5 p.m., and afterwards see their catch being auctioned.

 A tiny road leads down to the sandy beaches and picturesque bays which lie to the north of the village.

The scenery, which up to now has been quite rocky and uninviting, suddenly changes at the mouth of the Ebro. Its triangular-shaped delta juts out 30 km into the sea. Before you set out to explore this rather unusual landscape you should turn off at Aldea to the historic town of Tortosa which lies 13 km inland.

Tortosa Pop. 45,000; AA-40

This small commercial town, situated on the lower course of the Ebro, has no harbour but is the centre of the surrounding region of Baix Ebre.

 Tortosa's origins are lost in the mists of early Iberian history. The Romans Latinised the town, calling it Julia Augusta Dertosa, and even under the Goths and Arabs it was an important administrative and commercial centre. In the year 1148 it was captured by Berenguer IV, the Duke of Barcelona. In the 13th c. Tortosa boasted three harbours, on the river and the sea. The 'Costums de Tortosa' laid down in 1277 formed the basis of medieval Catalan civic law.

On several occasions the town was the seat of the Corts, the Aragón parliament, and in the 14th c. the famous *Controversias* took place here, when Pope Benedict XIII invited the rabbis of Aragón to take part in polemical discussions with Christian theologians. This was a unique event, which moved many Jews to embrace Christianity.

The town is still partly surrounded by its old walls and fortifications. The fortress itself, the *Castillo de la Zuda*

(*Castell de la Suda*), was recently restored. It lies on a flat, grass-covered hilltop alongside ruins from various historical periods. The thick fortified walls, as well as the part of the building where the Arab fort commanders lived, date back to the 10th c. The state-run hotel *Parador Nacional Castillo de la Zuda* is situated here today, and is a good example of one way in which ancient monuments can be successfully preserved.

From here it is only a few steps down to the large Gothic *cathedral* which was begun in the year 1347 and is one of the finest in Catalonia. Of the original Romanesque church only the interesting cloisters have survived; on the walls you can see monumental inscriptions which date from the 12th–15th c. Inside the cathedral you will see a colourful 14th c. Gothic winged altar behind the main altar. This is particularly impressive and is dedicated to the Virgen de las Estrellas. In a Baroque side-chapel there is an unusual statue of the Virgen de la Cinta. The belt (*la cinta*) is held in her hands.

Diagonally opposite the Baroque façade of the cathedral, towards the river, is the *Palacio Episcopal*, the Bishop's Palace, which dates back to the 14th c. and is another very good example of Catalan Gothic. The inner courtyard of the building is well worth viewing. Going past the cathedral again and along the Carrer dels Capellans, you will come to the *Real Colegio de San Luis* (royal school of St Louis), which was founded in the year 1544 by the Emperor Charles V for the education of young Moors. It later became a university, and today serves as the regional centre of the National Correspondence College. Inside, the Renaissance courtyard is enclosed by two-storeyed cloistered arcades, from which all the rooms lead off. Portraits in relief of the kings of Aragón from 1131 to 1621 decorate the walls.

Tortosa with the cathedral in the foreground

The former *Santo Domingo* (*Sant Domènec*) church is opposite the Colegio and forms part of the same architectural complex. The *Municipal Museum* is now housed here and contains archaeological finds and ceramics. The code of civic law already referred to is on display, together with a collection of oil paintings. It should be noted that the museum may be moved to another location in the near future. Both the school and the church are the work of the Tortosa master builder, Miquel Joan Anglés.

🍴 *Parador Nacional Castillo de la Zuda*; tel.(977) 44 44 50. *Racó del Mitg-Camí*, Ctra. Simpática 123; tel. (977) 44 31 48. *San Carlos*, c. Felipe Pedrell (fish dishes).

ℹ *Oficina Municipal de Turisme,* in the town hall, Plaza España s/n; tel. (977) 44 00 00.

The Ebro delta AA-40/41

The Ebro (Ebre) — the name comes from the word *Iberus* (Iberian) — is one of the longest rivers in Spain. For centuries the estuary has been silting up, causing the delta to grow larger year by year. The area is completely flat and intersected by waterways which carry

Rice-field in the Ebro delta

the river water to vast rice-fields. Here and there you come across lagoons, salt works and fish farms. In addition this intensively cultivated area offers the holidaymaker isolated sandy beaches which stretch for miles. Although totally lacking in amenities, they are paradise for those who simply wish to be alone. The best approach to the delta is by the road which branches off towards the sea 12 km north of Aldea (which is on the N-340). 10 km along this road, you come to the largest of the farming villages, *La Cava-Deltebre*.

Embarcador Olmos; tel. (977) 48 04 73. Trips down the Ebro to the estuary, every Sunday at 10 a.m. (approx. £3.50). Speed boats for water-skiing or delta trips (about £70 for a half day).

The two beaches *Playa Marquesa*, 5 km north (follow the signs), and *Playa Ríomar*, 10 km towards the estuary, are next to one another but with different access roads. They are very wide and together they stretch for almost 10 km. While Marquesa has not been developed, Ríomar has been somewhat built up, but this is not very visible from the beach.

Embarcador Olmos. A ferry (continuous service) crosses the Ebro from here for a charge of about 70p.

On the other side of the river is the small village of *San Jaime de Enveija* (Sant Jaume de l'Enveija) which may be reached by the ferry.

Playa de Eucaliptus, Playa del Trabucador. These beaches, approximately 10 km from San Jaime, may be reached by turning left immediately on leaving the landing stage. In the case of the former, there is a small development, and sometimes facilities are provided for water-sports. The Playa del Trabucador lies somewhat more to the south, on the spit of land which connects the Alfaques peninsula to the rest of the delta. These two beaches offer almost 20 km of sand and dunes.

By leaving the Playa de Eucaliptus on one of the three well signposted roads leading to the main N-340, you can get to the town of San Carlos.

San Carlos de la Rápita (Sant Carles de la Rápita) AA-41

This little fishing village to the south of the estuary was to have developed into one of the most significant harbours on the Spanish Mediterranean coast, a sea- and river-port connected to the Ebro by a canal. At least, that was what the liberal-minded Bourbon Charles III had in mind in 1781. Work on the project was commenced with enthusiasm, the canal was partly dredged, and the shells of the port buildings were already erected when the monarch died, and with him his plans for San Carlos. Only his name and the ruins of unfinished buildings remain as evidence of the ill-fated project. The town as it is today was developed in the 19th c.

Sandy beach to the south of the harbour. 10 km to the south you will find tiny inlets and at *Las Casas de Alcanar* a pebble beach.

 Pedalos.

Shellfish specialities: *Restaurante Miami*, Av. Constitució 37; tel. (977) 74 05 51. *Restaurante Fernandel*, Ctra. Barcelona Valencia; tel. (977) 74 03 58.

 Oficina de Turismo, Plaza Carlos III; tel. (977) 74 07 17.

Costa del Azáhar

The 'Orange-Blossom Coast' stretches from Vinaroz to Valencia. The first of the orange trees can be seen just before you reach Vinaroz, and in early summer the scent from their white flowers is intoxicating. Although they hardly ever ate the fruit, the Arabs always planted orange-trees in the inner courtyards of their mosques and palaces because of the aroma from the blossom, and it was they who gave the coast its name.

The orange plantations on the coastal plains border the road as far as Valencia. There are beaches here to suit everybody, while inland the rugged hills of the Maestrazgo, where the Knights of Montesa once ruled, tower over the countryside. If you are not worried by mountain roads, take one of the spectacular trips into the hinterland and follow in the tracks of medieval kings, knights and monks. The small dreamy towns and villages bear witness to a glorious past.

The Costa lies within the region of the old kingdom of Valencia which today forms part of an autonomous province of the same name. Valencia is bilingual. In addition to Castilian, Valencian, similar to Catalan but very much softer, is quite widely spoken.

Vinaroz (Vinaros) AA-42

This locally important seaport and trading centre is best known for the quality of its shellfish. It is well worth having a meal here.

How much the inhabitants feared the Berber pirates in the 16th c. is reflected in the thickness of the walls of the *Iglesia Parroquial* (parish church). The Baroque façade is the only graceful feature of the building.

The town's narrow, pebbly beach is bordered by an attractive Victorian promenade.

For shellfish: *Restaurante Casa Pacho*, c. San Gregorio; *Restaurante Machaco*, Paseo Marítimo.

i *Oficina Municipal de Turismo*, Plaza Jovellar; tel. (964) 45 08 14.

Benicarló AA-43

This is a small port with a lovely *parish church* which has two features typical of Valencia, a blue-tiled dome and an octagonal tower. Its Baroque façade is very similar to that of the church in Vinaroz.

There is a small sandy beach to the north of the harbour, and a pebble beach to the south. Adjoining this is a wide sandy beach which begins at the modern Parador Nacional, *Costa del Azáhar*. It is roughly 5 km long and stretches the length of the coastal road from Benicarló to Peñíscola.

   Pedalos.

✕ *Restaurante Can Vicent*, Ctra. Peñíscola; tel. (964) 47 10 06. *El*

Oranges on the 'Orange-Blossom Coast'

Flower-bedecked Peñíscola

king of Aragón. Between 1415 and 1424 the fortress was home to the Spanish antipope Benedict XIII. Because of the threat from the Turks, Philip II had the fortifications strengthened and extended in 1583 by the Italian architect Juan Bautista Antonelli. It is true that the Turkish fleet had been defeated at Lepanto in 1571, but their North African allies, the Berbers, continued to make the Spanish Mediterranean coast unsafe with their acts of piracy.

📷 The *Castillo* itself is in relatively good condition, as during the various French wars Peñíscola did not suffer the same devastation as the rest of the region. On the other hand, some damage was inflicted during the civil wars, but this has, in the main, been put right through intelligent and tasteful restoration. It is best to park your car beneath the ramparts and enter the town through its massive gateway, the work of the Escorial architect Juan Herrera. At the top of the gate you can

Cortijo, Méndez Núñez s/n; tel. (964) 47 00 75. *Marynton,* Paseo Marítimo s/n; tel. (964) 47 30 11.

ℹ️ *Oficina Municipal de Turismo,* Plaza San Andrés s/n; tel. (964) 47 31 80.

Peñíscola Pop. 10,000; AA-43
The name means peninsula but, oddly enough, from whichever side you approach the town you will always see the semicircular 60-m-high rock and never the spit of land which leads to it. The white walls of its 600 houses sparkle in the sunshine above the magnificent battlements, and above the houses, as a finishing touch, stands the majestic Castillo.

🐎 The stronghold was erected in the 13th c. by the Knights Templar, and in 1319 was handed over to the Knights of the Order of Montesa by the

see the Habsburg crest. A steep flight of steps takes you through another gate (adorned with the crest of Pope Benedict XIII) into the fortress itself. This innermost and oldest part of the fortress is a remarkable example of the military architecture of the late Middle Ages. Unfortunately the rooms and halls are unfurnished and one has to use one's imagination to visualise the life in exile of the stubborn and embittered Benedict XIII. He could not accept his dismissal at the Council of Constance and retired here.

At the centre of the castle complex is the courtyard, one side of which overlooks the sea. From here, as well as from the various towers and terraces, the view is unrivalled — and you can certainly feel the breeze blowing! The hall used as a basilica by the pope overlooks the courtyard. Next to it is a gloomy flight of steps which leads down to the room where the Conclave took place in 1423. The austerity of the surroundings makes a strong impression, particularly when compared with the splendour of the papal palaces in Rome or Avignon. At the same time, you are conscious of just how much the obstinate antipope believed in the justice of his cause.

Built against the walls of the fortress, on the highest point of the promontory, is the pilgrimage church of *Virgen Ermitaña* which has a very fine Baroque façade dating from 1708. The town itself is made up of steep narrow streets lined with relatively modern houses. The Moorish influence is apparent in their flat roofs and whitewashed walls.

Hostería de Mar on the coastal road to Benicarló, with a fine view over the peninsula. *Casa Severino*, Urb. Las Atalayas; *Casa Jaime*, Paseo Marítimo; *Casa Vicente*, opposite the castle.

Virgen Ermitaña: festival of the patron saint in early September.

Peñíscola

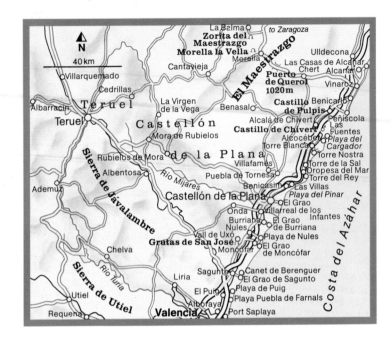

Folk-dancing and mock battles between 'Christians' and 'Moors', in period costume.

 Pedalos.

 Las Atalayas development.

 Teatro, Arjub, Salam.

 Surfing, Av. Papa Luna; *Trilogy*, c. Vicente Blasco Ibáñez 16; *La Fleca*, Plaza Ayuntamiento.

i *Centro de Iniciativas Turísticas*, Paseo Marítimo s/n; tel. (964) 48 02 08.

🚌 Excursions into the hinterland

After passing through wild countryside you reach the hinterland of the Maestrazgo, which from the 13th–16th c. was ruled first by the Knights Templar and then by the Knights of the Order of Montesa. From Vinaroz take the main N-232 road heading west towards Zaragoza. Although well constructed the road is full of bends as it winds its way up to the *Puerto de Querol* pass at 1020 m. From here you will get your first glimpse of the town and castle of Morella. The scenery is desolate but at the same time impressive. One indication of the attempt by man to reap some benefit from this barren region can be seen in the many stone walls, constructed by the farmers from the millions of stones which lay scattered over their land.

Morella Pop. 2600

The town is situated on a steep hill and is surrounded by 14th c. walls which stretch for more than 2 km and are very well preserved. Above them rises a gigantic castle rock crowned by the ruins of the fortress.

Altar of Santa María, Morella

Six gates are built into the enormous walls. If you follow the access road you come to the two finest, *San Mateo* and *San Miguel*. It is best to leave your car by the San Miguel Gate and explore the town from there on foot. Once through the gate take the third street on the left. This forms the longitudinal axis of the town and its first section is called Juan Giner Street. The *Ayuntamiento* (town hall) is situated on the left; it dates from the 15th c. and has Renaissance modifications.

The main street continues as *Blasco de Aragón* and is lined on both sides with fine arcades. A market is held there under the arches every Thursday and Sunday. Where the arcades end you will see on the left a Gothic mansion, once the residence of the Ram family but now converted into a hotel.

At this point make a sharp turn to the right, which brings you to the *Plaza Benedicto XV*. Here against the castle rock is the 14th c. church of *Santa María*. Owing to lack of space the main doorways of the church were built next to each other in the façade looking on to the square. It is said that two stonemasons, father and son, had a bet as they worked away with their chisels, one carving each doorway. Whoever made the larger one, the *Puerta de los Apóstoles* on the right-hand side, was undoubtedly the winner, as it is by far the more splendid of the two. A unique example of church architecture is to be found inside: the *coro* (choir), which is normally built in the centre of the nave and blocks out the view of the high altar, is in this church raised on four pillars high above the heads of the worshippers. This enables the congregation to follow visually the service taking place at the altar. Access to the choir is by a spiral staircase richly decorated with reliefs. It winds its way around one of the supporting pillars and is a masterpiece of 15th c. stonemasonry.

When you leave the church, turn right and it is only a few steps to the former Franciscan Monastery (*Convento de San Francisco*). Today the monastery, which lies at the foot of the castle, is in ruins, but the elegant archways of the 14th c. cloisters are still standing, and there is a good view from here up to the castle. From the monastery you can climb up to the ruins of the fortress where you will have superb views in every direction.

In the former mansion of the Ram family, Hotel *Cardenal Ram*, Cuesta Suñer 1; tel. (964) 16 00 00.

At the end of August, every sixth year (1994), *Virgen de Vallivana*, an extravagant festival lasting a full two weeks, with medieval folk-dancing in costume, and a procession with the statue of Mary from the pilgrimage church of Vallivana to Morella (8 km).

Centro de Iniciativas Turísticas, Torre de San Miguel; tel. (964) 16 01 25.

The whole of the Maestrazgo is riddled with caves, which are evidence of a thriving settlement here in the Stone Age. The most accessible caves are at *Morella la Vella*, 8 km from Morella itself, and are worth visiting for the splendid paintings from this period which are to be found on the walls. The caves at *Zorita del Maestrazgo*, 20 km away on the N-232 in the direction of Zaragoza, are of ritual significance. In the 14th c. a pilgrimage church, *Santuario de la Balma*, was hewn out of the rocks here.

 September 8th, *pilgrimage from Zorita* to this sanctuary. As part of the ceremony in the Santuario de la Balma, a duel takes place between an angel and a devil, both played by people from the village.

There is no made-up coastal road between Peñíscola and the next town of Alcocéber. However, if you are prepared to risk your car, you can go via narrow country lanes southwards from Peñíscola or northwards from Alcocéber to a few isolated sandy inlets. The N-340 and the A-7 wind around the Sierra de Hirta, past the ruins of two castles, the Castillo de Pulpis and the Castillo de Chivert. Opposite the latter castle lies *Alcalá de Chivert*, whose typically Valencian octagonal bell-tower can be seen from miles away. At 60 m it is the highest in the whole region.

Alcocéber (Alcossebre) AA-44

Situated 5 km from the N-340, Alcocéber used to be an unimportant little fishing village. It has now, however, been built up quite tastefully into a thriving holiday centre. Several beaches were made accessible, a marina, hotels and restaurants were built — and all this without the towering apartment blocks and high-rise developments which are so often packed together in holiday resorts. Alcocéber is still comparatively quiet, ideal for children and with much to offer the tourist.

 Las Fuentes, close to the development of the same name with a yacht marina; *El Cargador*, below the town; *La Romana*, the most southerly and isolated beach. All have fine sand.

To the south of Alcocéber the following beaches may be reached via small lanes which lead off the N-340. *Torre Nostra,* the beach belonging to the village of Torre Blanca which lies further inland, has not been commercially developed and consists more of pebbles than of sand. *Torre de la Sal* is approached through a camp site which is well signposted, and is a lovely sandy beach, behind which is a rather run-down but picturesque fishing village.

 A huge water-chute with four separate slides, each 100 m in length. *Turbogan Acuático* (water tobogganing) contests between this village and Las Fuentes.

 Apart from the usual entertainment in Alcocéber itself, there is the lively *El Túnel* to the south of the Playa Romana, housed in the ruins of an old fortress.

Oropesa del Mar AA-45

The town consists of two sections. One is a village lying inland and situated in the shadow of a ruined castle, and the other a fairly large seaside resort stretching out on each side of *Cape Oropesa*, which is crowned by a 15th c. watch-tower, *Torre del Rey*.

 To the north of the cape, the long, immaculate sandy beach *Morro del Gos* (dog's snout!); to the south, in a shell-shaped bay, the short but very wide beach *Playa de la Concha*.

Pedalos.

Clubs *Europesa*, *Agave* and *Boramar*.

Benicasim

 *Bolera Farito*, Ctra. Faro 90.

 *Talleres Mediterráneo*, Av. de la Plana 99.

🏍 South of the town, just before the turning to Benicasim.

❌ *El Mervi*, Paseo Marítimo Mediterráneo 18; *El Blasori*, Ctra. Faro 76; *Doña Resu*, Paseo Marítimo La Concha 26.

✖ *Mesón Cueva*, Pl. Constitución 4; *La Parilla*, c. Onésimo Redondo 26.

🍷 *Hollywood*, Ctra. Faro 87; *La Bohemia*, Ctra. Faro 91.

🎵 *UFO's*, c. Almería s/n; *Babyo*, Ctra. Faro 3.

ℹ *Centro de Iniciativas Turísticas*, Av. Plana 4; tel. (964) 31 00 20.

The N-340 forks a little way south of Oropesa; you should take the coastal route, which leads to the harbour of the provincial capital *Castellón*. Only a few rocky inlets separate the towns of Oropesa and Benicasim.

Benicasim (Benicéssim) AA-45

This is the largest holiday resort on the Orange-Blossom Coast. Here you will find every kind of amusement you could wish for, in pleasant surroundings. In spite of its size Benicasim is not oppressive or overwhelming. The best sandy beach begins in the south of the resort. The northern suburb of *Heliópolis*, however, has only a few small bays and inlets.

⛵ Pedalos.

🏄 At Heliópolis.

🔫 🔍 🏍 On the N-340 near Oropesa.

🚲 At the Hotel *Orange*, Gran Avenida.

✖ *Torreón Bernat*, Av. Ferrándiz Salvador; *Plaza*, c. Colón 4; *La Estrada*, Av. Castellón (Italian).

🍷 *Brighton*, Av. Castellón; *Niú*, Ctra. Santa Águeda.

🎵 *Takeno's*, Gran Avenida.

ℹ *Centro de Iniciativas Turísticas*, Ayuntamiento, c. Médico Segarra 30; tel. (964) 30 02 81.

🚌 To the Carmelite Monastery of *Desierto de las Palmas*, 10 km away. The chain of hills which rises up to the north of Benicasim is named after the monastery and means literally 'the desert of palms'. The word 'desert', however, is not used in its geographical sense. In Spain Carmelite monasteries have always been called that, in order to convey their utter seclusion from the world. There really are palm trees, however, in the monastery garden.

The monastery, built in 1694, is plain yet beautiful and of the same shade of red as the surrounding hills. The view over Benicasim and the sea below is truly breathtaking. The exhibits in a small museum compensate for the unattractive monastery chapel. In addition to several paintings the museum can boast documents signed by the founder of the order, St Theresa of Ávila, as well as a beautiful Gothic statue of the Madonna, known as Nuestra Señora de la Alegría, Our Lady of Joy. In the souvenir shop you can buy the proverbially good monastery liqueur.

The road from Benicasim to the harbour of Castellón is flanked by a long, very inviting beach of fine sand, which is at its best near the Flying Club. Here it is known as the *Playa del Pinar* and is fringed by pine woods and stylish villas.

 Pedalos.

  Hotel de Golf.

 Restaurante Xaloc.

 El Pirata, Hotel de Golf.

Soon afterwards you reach *El Grao*, the harbour district of the provincial capital, which is so attractively and neatly laid out that it looks as if a landscape gardener had planned it. It is 4 km back inland to Castellón de la Plana.

Castellón de la Plana (Castelló)
Pop. 125,000; AA-46
Castellón can boast neither great heroes nor any particular monuments. The

town embodies the spirit of the Valencian coastal people, who are industrious, down-to-earth, honest citizens. The inhabitants of the town and surrounding areas make a living mostly from the large orange-plantations and from the manufacture of porcelain and ceramics.

Castellón is one of the towns which was badly damaged during the Civil War of 1936–39. Many of the old churches have been rebuilt stone by stone, including the *Cathedral of Santa María* (Gothic, with Renaissance features) which stands in the attractive Plaza Mayor. Here, too, stands the 17th c. bell-tower *El Fadrí*, built in the same style as the Miguelete tower in Valencia. The *town hall* dates from the same period and has also been completely restored.

A *museum* has been set up in the *Palacio Provincial*, the seat of the provincial administration, in the Plaza María Augustina. It contains paintings by Spanish masters of the 16th–18th c., including Francisco Ribalta and Ribera. You should also visit the Capuchin convent (*Convento de Capuchinas*), at Calle Núñez de Arce 5, as it has some attractive Baroque tiles and pictures of the saints. These are attributed to Zurbarán, but are probably only copies or were painted by his pupils.

 Castellón: *Fiesta de la Magdalena*, in the 3rd week of Lent; processions, pilgrimage, dancing, fireworks, street theatre. El Grao: last week in June, 'toros embolados' (see page 15) on the beach, dancing, etc.

Club de Tenis Castellón; c. Donación, between the town and El Grao.

Bolera La Plana, c. Vázquez Mella 36, Castellón.

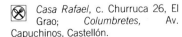 *Casa Rafael*, c. Churruca 26, El Grao; *Columbretes*, Av. Capuchinos, Castellón.

Club Nautico, Muelle Poniente, El Grao.

 Scandals, c. Lagasca 3; *El Hostal,* c. Méndez Núñez 9.

 Bianco, c. Gobernador 65, Castellón; *Valentino,* Ramón y Cajal 23, Castellón; *Varadero,* Av. Buenavista 45, El Grao.

 Información Turística, Pl. María Augustina 5, Castellón; tel. (964) 22 77 03.

To **Onda**, 30 km away, to visit the Natural History Museum. Head towards Valencia on the N-340 and turn inland at Villarreal on to the C-228. Once you get to Onda follow the signs to the *Museo de ciencias naturales 'El Carmen'.* Here, with the assistance of their fellow brothers from all over the world, the Carmelites have amassed a remarkable collection of stuffed animals. Children will really enjoy themselves here. The only drawback is that the exhibits are all labelled in Spanish and Latin. Opening times: daily except Monday, 9.30 a.m.–2 p.m. and 3.30–7 p.m.

To the mountain village of **Villafamés** 25 km away. Take the C-238 to Puebla de Tarnesa and there turn left. Situated in the foothills of the Sierra de Engarcerán, Villafamés with its castle towers over a fertile plain. The charms of the village have inspired many an artist, so that today, in addition to the original farming community, a large colony of artists forms part of village life. As a direct result of their presence the widely acclaimed Museum of Modern Art (*Museo de Arte Contemporáneo*) was opened in the Palacio del Bayle (open daily 11 a.m.– 1 p.m. and 5–7 p.m.). Rather less appropriately situated — for no wine is produced here — is the wine museum (*Museo del Vino*; enquire in the Art Museum). Absorb the village atmosphere. Stroll through the narrow streets and alleyways, and in the

coolness of the evening have a glass of wine in one of the bars.

The small village of Burriana lies to the south of Castellón on the other side of the Río Mijares. You can reach it by turning off towards the sea just outside Villarreal.

Burriana AA-48

This village is surrounded by orange-plantations. The export of fruit for the entire area is handled by its harbour, *El Grao.* Only a few of the beaches around the harbour are sandy; shingle predominates here. Along the promenade there are a large number of attractive holiday villas dating from the 1920s when Burriana was a very fashionable resort.

 Oficina Municipal de Turismo, c. Iturbi 33; tel. (964) 51 15 40.

A special tip

The caves of San José (*Grutas de San José*) in the village of *Vall de Uxó* will open up a whole new subterranean world for you, complete with a navigable river of over a kilometre in length. The lighting in the grottos is very effective, so that during the boat trip the full beauty of the stalagmites and stalactites may be enjoyed.

Next you come to the small towns of *Nules* and *Moncófar* whose beaches are accessible not only via country lanes from Grao de Burriana but also from the N-340.

However, apart from the approach through the orange-groves, there is very little else of interest. You may be able to find an unspoilt piece of beach, but it will not be of the finest sand.

Sagunto (Sagunt or Morvedre)
Pop. 60,000; AA-51

The ancient Greeks established a trading post in *Zakynthos,* but true fame came to Sagunto when it triggered

Roman amphitheatre, Sagunto

the Second Punic War. The town lay within the region over which Carthage had influence, and in the year 219 B.C. its citizens refused to open their gates to Hannibal, the Carthaginian general. Instead they appealed to Rome for help, but nothing came except consolatory messages. In the meantime, Hannibal mercilessly laid siege to the town. For many months the inhabitants withstood the onslaught, and as they were not prepared to surrender they finally set fire to their town; many of them perished in the flames. The few survivors were then massacred by Hannibal's soldiers. After Rome finally defeated Carthage Sagunto was rebuilt as *Muri Veteres* (Ancient Walls).

The ancient ruins lie at the foot of the former fortress high above the New Town. Below the Roman amphitheatre is a small *archaeological museum* (open from 9 a.m.–8 p.m.) in which are displayed artefacts from the last 2000 years. The amphitheatre itself, which is in a good state of preservation, was extended by the Romans to accommodate 8000 spectators on its 33 tiers. The magnificent view over the plain and the sea provides a wonderful backdrop for the stage. Even today you can still appreciate the perfect acoustics of the amphitheatre. (Opening times: 4–8 p.m.)

Further up you come to the ruins of the fortress, which has spanned a long period of Spanish history. As late as the beginning of the last century, during the French occupation, one of Napoleon's commanders, Marshal Suchet, had the walls repaired. Since then, however, there have been three civil wars which destroyed almost everything once again. The part which is the best preserved is the massive *Puerta de Almenara*, a gate dating back to Moorish times, which can be found between the two eastern ranges of the building.

The lower part of the town is in the main modern and unattractive. Nevertheless, the principal church, *Santa María* (1334), in the Plaza Mayor, is worth a visit. It was set on fire in 1936 during the Civil War, which proved unexpectedly beneficial, as the

Gothic façade which up to that time had been hidden under Baroque plaster was fully revealed. A rare example of Valencian early Gothic (in fact still almost Romanesque in appearance) is the *Church of San Salvador*, in the east of the town, on the square of the same name. Finally you should visit the chapel of *San Miguel* in the Calle Mayor. It was built in the 18th c. and has a carved inscription over the doorway which, when translated, reads roughly: 'The devil cannot enter here, as he would have St Michael to fear.'

 El Grao de Sagunto has a sandy beach, but owing to its proximity to the harbour this is not really to be recommended. A few kilometres north, however, there is a beautiful sandy beach at *Canet de Berenguer* which as yet has not become overpopulated. This can be reached by a small coastal road with a bridge over the Río Palancia or alternatively by a little turning off the N-340. The simple restaurants near the beach are specially recommended for fish dishes and paella.

El Puig

This suburban town lies a short distance south of Sagunto and is looked upon as the gateway to Valencia. It is dominated by a huge monastery. A fortress built on the *puig* (hill) defended Valencia at the time of Moorish rule, and El Cid and James the Conqueror of Aragón both had to fight fiercely for this key position before the town surrendered to them. In the crucial battle against the Arabs, King James was so unexpectedly victorious that even the most respected chroniclers of the day came to the conclusion that St George himself had come to the assistance of the Christians. In gratitude the king had a monastery erected here, which was later modified in the 16th and 17th c. in the austere style of the Escorial. Occupation by the French, civil wars and the secularisation of church property all contributed to the

loss of the monastery's legendary wealth. All that remains is a granite statue of the Virgin Mary, the *Mare de Deu del Puig*, by the Florentine sculptor Pisano, a precursor of Donatello. Mary is revered as the patron saint of the region of Valencia. A short tour through this immense building would be worth while. Even today, it serves as a residence for the Spanish royal family when they are in Valencia. (Open: 10 a.m.–1 p.m. and 4–7 p.m.)

 About 1 km from the town is the *Playa de Puig*, the southern part of which is modestly commercialised and has a most attractive sandy beach. Before you get to Valencia there are two other bathing beaches at *Playa Puebla de Farnals*, which also has a yacht marina. Here there is one tower block after another, as these beaches are very popular with the Valencians at the weekends.

 Pedalos.   **S**

 Oficina Municipal de Turismo; tel. (96) 1 44 05 41.

Port Saplaya

You can reach this town by taking the Alboraya motorway exit. In the pretty little marina the yachts moor directly in front of the houses.

 A wide sandy beach stretches all the way to the harbour in Valencia. Access is only from Port Saplaya or from the harbour. In order to find a quiet spot it is thus worth walking a little way along the beach.

 Restaurante Club Nautico; De Silvi (Italian).

 Mosqueteros; Horchatería Toni.

On the *Plaza Mayor;* tel. (96) 3 71 36 11.

Valencia Pop. 750,000

The old city centre is bordered in the north by the dried-up river-bed of the Turia — the river water is diverted for the irrigation of orange-groves and rice-fields. A ring road consisting of the streets Calles Colón, Játiva and Guillén de Castro now skirts the centre in place of the city walls. The area within this ring road may be explored comfortably on foot as nowhere is it more than 2 km across. It should be quite easy to take in all the places of interest in the city in one day, but if you want to view the museums a little more thoroughly then you should allow half a day longer.

The city was founded by the Romans in the year 138 B.C. It was first inhabited by veterans of the Roman armies; hence its name which means 'the Valiant'. Christianity came to Valencia as long ago as the 1st century and it was the Apostle St James, whom the Spaniards call Santiago, who appointed the first bishop — Eusebius.

However, the Christians were continually being persecuted. The Deacon Vinzenz was martyred in the 4th c., was later canonised and has since been one of the city's patron saints.

Then the period of the invasions began. First came the Goths whose rule lasted for 300 years, followed by the Arabs who arrived in 711 and stayed for

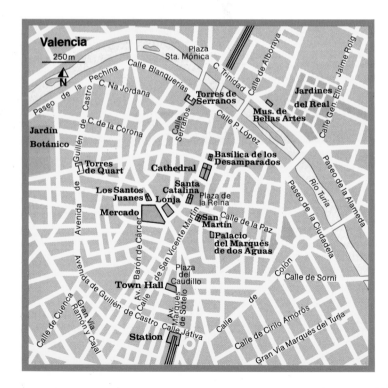

Palacio del Marqués de dos Aguas

half a millennium. It was the Arabs who were responsible for Valencia's wealth; they not only developed the irrigation systems required for the cultivation of oranges and rice, but also installed kilns for the manufacture of tiles and ceramics.

In 1238 James I, king of neighbouring Aragón, conquered the city, of which El Cid had already gained control for a few years at the end of the 11th c. Linked as it was to Aragón, Valencia participated in the former's expansion in the Mediterranean. It rose to be one of the major cities in Spain, until it was brought to the edge of ruin in 1609 when Arab craftsmen and labourers, the Moriscos, were expelled from the country. In the War of the Spanish Succession at the beginning of the 18th c. Valencia supported the Archduke Charles, and for that reason was punished by the victorious Bourbons by the withdrawal of its autonomous privileges.

El Cid, the hero of Valencia

The knight went to see the money-lenders, accompanied by two servants who placed a heavy chest, reinforced with iron, on the ground. 'This contains golden treasure,' he declared, 'and I would like a loan granted on it.' The two money-lenders nodded agreement. 'But on one condition,' continued the knight, 'that the chest remains locked, now and for a whole year. Only if I have not repaid my loan by that time may you open the chest. You must swear that you will obey my instructions.'

The money-lenders gave it some thought and then decided; after all, their new customer was not just anybody but El Cid himself, the hero of countless battles and conquests. So they gave him their word and paid out the money.

They had made the right decision. Before the year was up, El Cid appeared, this time laden with booty, for in the meantime he had invaded and plundered a neighbouring Moorish principality, as was customary practice at that time. He repaid the debt and his servants shouldered the heavy chest. The chronicles do not say whether El Cid gave orders for the chest to be opened on the spot so that the money-lenders might see inside, but they do say that it contained nothing but sand.

That is how the story goes in the epic poem 'El Cantar de Mío Cid', written around 1150 and transmitted to us through Corneille's tragedy.

'Cid' was the respectful name which the Arabs gave to this great adversary; it comes from the word 'Sidi' which is the equivalent of 'Lord'. His real name was Rodrigo Díaz de Vivar and he was a vassal of the Castilian crown. He was also one of the most courageous warriors and clever commanders of his time. He hailed from Burgos where he also lies buried, and against one of the walls of the cathedral you can see to this day the famous chest. But historically speaking, he belongs to Valencia, as it was he who conquered the city towards the end of the 11th c. It was not yet won for good, however, as after his death the Moors regained their independence. The short years of his rule over Valencia, however, were of historic significance: the advance on Aragón and Catalonia by the Moors was prevented. As a great personality, of course, El Cid does not belong to Valencia alone. The whole of Spain looks to this model of a fearless knight who was at the same time a faithful husband and caring father. His two daughters married well into Christian aristocratic families. He remained fanatically loyal to his own king, of Castile, even though the monarch treated him disgracefully and from time to time even banished him from the country.

The city's treasures

The city gates: Of the old city walls only two pairs of monumental towers still remain: the *Torres de Quart* in the west, and the *Torres de Serranos* in the north. Both were built in the 14th c. to defend the city gates. The ancient city centre is best approached through the Torres de Serranos. In the towers themselves is a small *maritime museum* which, with its fine collection of model ships, offers a welcome change, especially to youngsters, after sightseeing in the town. (Open: 10 a.m.–2 p.m.; closed Mondays.)

Government Palace: The Calle Serranos leads to the Plaza Manises in the centre of the administrative district. Here stands the Government Palace, the *Palau de la Generalitat,* a lovely Gothic building, the main section of which was begun in the 15th c. The towers were added in the 16th and 19th c. respectively, but nevertheless blend in beautifully with the whole. Originally built to serve as the seat of the legislative assembly, the Cortes, of the kingdom of Valencia, the palace is today home to the autonomous regional government. Inside you will find a splendid arcaded courtyard, a Baroque chapel and the 16th c. *Salón de las Cortes*, with a magnificent coffered ceiling and interesting frescos which portray a meeting of the legislative assembly. The *Cambra Dorada* (Golden Chamber), so called because of the splendour of its gilded ceiling, is today the office of the head of government. The palace also contains a fine collection of works by Valencian late Impressionists.

Basílica de los Desamparados: It is just a short walk from the Plaza Manises to the Plaza de la Virgen where stand the two most important churches in Valencia. Overlooking the Plaza is the basilica of the *Virgen de los Desamparados*, the Virgin of the Helpless, who is revered as the patroness of the city. The plain Baroque church was built between 1652 and 1667 under the direction of the architect Martínez Ponce de Urriana. The ground-plan is oval and the domed ceiling is decorated with a fresco by Angel Palomino (1701) representing the Glory of Heaven. High up on the wall behind the high altar stands an almost life-size statue of the Virgin which dates from the beginning of the 15th c. and is the work of an unknown sculptor.

The cathedral: This is diagonally opposite the Basílica de los Desamparados. The first building work was commissioned by El Cid in the year 1095, when he had the Moorish mosque which stood here converted into a Christian church. Prior to that — as is so often the case in Mediterranean areas — a Roman temple and then a Visigothic church had stood on this site. The

Valencia — the city of El Cid

present-day cathedral goes back to the 13th and 14th c. In spite of that, however, the Gothic character of the exterior is not immediately noticeable as it has been extended and altered in a variety of styles. A tour of the church should begin at the Gothic doorway, *Puerta de los Apóstoles*, which is the

Cathedral doorway

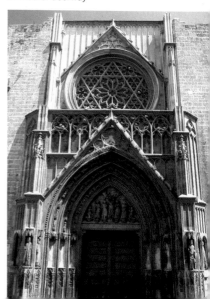

Torre del Miguelete, Valencia

(pretender to the throne in the War of the Spanish Succession).

Next to the main façade is the octagonal bell-tower known as *Micalet* or *Miguelete*, which stands about 50 m high. The tower, which is one of Valencia's landmarks, dates from 1381 and can be climbed via a narrow, rather alarming spiral staircase of 207 steps.

The cathedral's interior has been stripped of its Baroque adornments and is now once again an example of light, airy Gothic. The windows are glazed with wafer-thin alabaster, which considerably enhances the effect of the lighting. The winged main altar, which depicts scenes from the life of Christ, dates from the 16th c. and is by the Valencian artists Yañez de la Almedina and Hernando de los Llanos, who were obviously strongly influenced by the Florentine School, and in particular by Leonardo da Vinci.

Of the many side chapels you should make a point of visiting the one dedicated to the Holy Grail (*Capilla del Santo Cáliz*), in which is displayed a cup popularly believed to be that used by Christ at the Last Supper. The vessel is made of agate and the stem and handles are the work of a Byzantine goldsmith, while the base which was added later is made from a shell with pearls and precious stones. The relic is kept on a superb Renaissance alabaster altar created by the Florentine Poggibonsi. To the left of this altar, which depicts scenes from the Bible, you can see massive iron chains on the wall — war trophies claimed by King Alfonso the Magnanimous. They are the chains from the harbour at Marseilles which he had to break through in 1423 in order to plunder the town. In the *cathedral museum* you can see some very good paintings by the Valencian School of the 15th–17th c., as well as two pictures by Goya of St Francis Borgia. (Open: Monday–Saturday 10 a.m.–1 p.m.; in the summer months also from 4–6 p.m.)

work of the 14th c. French master Nicholas of Autun. After that, on the left-hand side, comes the so-called New Chapter House, *Obra Nueva del Cabildo*, with a wonderful arcaded Renaissance gallery which gives the whole area a Roman atmosphere. It was designed in 1566 by the stonemason Miguel Porcar. By going through the Romanesque doorway (the *Puerta de la Almoina*) you will arrive at the Baroque main façade, which dates from 1703 and is the work of Konrad Rudolf, a German pupil of Bernini and court sculptor to the Archduke Charles

Santa Catalina and San Martín:
Diagonally opposite the main façade of
the cathedral and towering over the city
is the hexagonal church tower of Santa
Catalina which dates back to the late
17th c. and is well worth seeing. The
church was gutted by fire in the Civil War
and unfortunately was not very
attractively restored. A little further on, if
you walk down the Calle San Vicente
Martín, you will see on the façade of the
Church of San Martín a very impressive
statue of the saint by the Flemish
sculptor Peter de Beckere (1494).

Plaza Redonda: Immediately to the right
lies the Plaza Redonda, an architectural
oddity dating from 1831, when an
attempt was made to organise the street
traders under one roof. Instead of
operating anywhere on the market place
as in the past, they were compelled to
trade from little shops within this
structure. These still exist today and give
a semi-rural atmosphere to the activity
on the square.

Lonja and Consolat de Mar: A few
blocks away you will come to the proper
market place, the *Plaza del Mercado*. On
one side, majestically dominating the
square, is the huge *Lonja* or *Llotja de
Seda* (silk exchange). Nowhere in the
whole of Valencia is there a finer
example of secular Gothic architecture.
The architect, Pere Compte, was also
responsible for the Palau de la
Generalitat and for parts of the
cathedral. The main façade, in three
parts, has a tower in the centre, the
Torreón, which can be ascended by a
splendid spiral staircase. From the top
you can enjoy a panoramic view of the
city. The left wing of the exchange
houses the large, well proportioned
trading hall, *Salón de Contrataciones*,
with twenty-four twisted columns. It was
here in the Middle Ages that the world-
famous Valencian silk trade was carried
on.

In the extension on the right of the
exchange building, designed by the
same architect, was the seat of the
Consolat de Mar which was founded in
the year 1283 and was the first maritime
court in Europe. Its great influence
mirrored the dominant position which
the kingdom of Aragón enjoyed at that
time in the whole of the Mediterranean.
The colourful 14th c. coffered ceiling
with beautifully carved ornamentation is
famous. It was originally in the old town
hall which was demolished in the last
century.

Los Santos Juanes: On the opposite side
of the market place stands the 17th c.
church *Iglesia de los Santos Juanes*. The
plain façade is dominated by two huge
doorways with a stone relief of the Virgin
Mary, a work of the same period by the
Italian sculptor Jacobo Bartessi. Inside,
the dome is painted with frescos by
Angel Palomino which are somewhat
reminiscent of those in the Sistine
Chapel.

Next to the church is the market hall,
in which the excessive use of iron
supports is a typical feature of the
Victorian era.

**Palacio del Marqués de dos Aguas and
the Ceramics Museum:** The palace is
a magnificent example of Valencian
Baroque. To reach it, go back to the
Church of San Martín and from there
walk a little way up the Calle Abadía de
San Martín. The design of this town
house is by the architect Hipólito Rovira
Brocandel. The most extraordinary
feature of its façade is the fanciful
alabaster doorway worked in 1740 by
Vergara. It is crowned by a Madonna and
is so overloaded with complicated motifs
that the overall impression is almost
overpowering.

The palace houses the best collection
of ceramics in the whole of Spain and
this should not be missed. Particularly
attractive are the painted and glazed

tiles, the *azulejos*, so named after their original blue colour (*azul* = azure). Azulejos portraying popular scenes decorated entire walls, just as they do in the 18th c. Valencian kitchen which may be seen in the museum.

You can also see plates by modern masters such as Picasso and the Valencian Benlliure. As well as the ceramics there are also Rococo carriages, Baroque furniture, and national costumes and court dress. (Open: Tuesday to Saturday 10 a.m.–2 p.m., 4–6 p.m.)

Museo de Bellas Artes: This is considered to be one of the finest museums in Spain. It is situated in the Academy of Fine Arts on the far side of the river Turia. The museum is devoted almost exclusively to artists of the Valencian School who, as a consequence of Valencia's situation on the Mediterranean, were strongly influenced by Italian art. In addition to the period between the 14th and 17th c., Valencia once again made a great name for itself at the end of the 19th c. when the town became the centre of Spanish Late Impressionism. A whole floor in the museum is given over to this period. Sculptures, archaeological finds and mosaics are on display on the ground floor and in the courtyard.

The first floor is given over almost entirely to works by Valencian artists. There are very fine Gothic winged altars, mostly created by unknown hands, and triptychs by the best Spanish artists of the late Gothic period, such as Pere Nicolau, Lorenzo Zaragoza and Jacomart. The Valencian Renaissance is represented by Yañez de la Almedina and Hernando de los Llanos, Vicente Macip and his son Juan de Juanes, Borrás, Orrente and Osona. Valencia's Baroque painters de Zariñena, Ribera, Ribalta, Esteban March and Espinosa also enjoyed great renown. In addition there are pictures by Murillo and

Zurbarán, and the celebrated self-portrait by Velázquez. From the early 19th c. there are portraits and sketches by Goya.

Almost all the works exhibited on the second floor are by the Valencian Impressionists and other artists of the 19th c. They include Joaquín Sorolla, Ignacio Pinazo, Muñoz Degrain and José Benlliure. (Open: Tuesday to Saturday 10 a.m.–2 p.m., 4–6 p.m.; Sunday 10 a.m.–2 p.m.)

The Ayuntamiento (town hall): Situated on the main square, *Plaza del Caudillo* or *del País Valenciano*, the town hall was built in the late 19th c. Inside you will find the *Museo Municipal* (Municipal Museum) which contains interesting documents relating to the history of the city. The standard with which James I entered the newly conquered city in 1238 is on display, as well as the Code of Civic Rights dated 1329 and the exchange table from the Municipal Bank, which was founded as long ago as 1407. Here you can see, in the original, the oldest bill of exchange in the world, bearing the date February 19th 1376. In addition, the museum has a good collection of paintings of the Baroque period, several items by the local artist and pupil of Goya Vicente López, and a representative selection of works by Valencian Impressionists. (Open: weekdays 9 a.m.–1 p.m.)

Estacion del Norte: Not far from the Plaza del Caudillo, down the Avenida Marqués de Sotelo, connoisseurs of Art Nouveau will find a real feast for their eyes — the railway station, one of the finest examples of this architectural style in Spain. It was built between 1909 and 1917 by Demetrio Ribes. The pinnacles on the façade are decorated with glazed ceramic reliefs depicting orange-branches and the Valencian imperial arms. The booking-office which is lined from floor to ceiling with mosaics is also very attractive. In the cafeteria, the former waiting room, you can still admire lovely examples of Valencian hand-produced tiles in Art Deco style. The scenes from everyday life are based on designs by José Benlliure.

 You will find every conceivable article for sale at the huge *Sunday flea-market* which is held on the Plaza de Nápoles y Sicilia and in the adjoining streets as far as the Plazas de Zaragoza and del Caudillo — furniture and pottery as well as the usual bric-a-brac. Antique-shops also open on a Sunday. On Sunday mornings art auctions are held in the *Círculo de Bellas Artes*, Calle Moratín, and entrance is free. There is a stamp- and coin-market in the *Lonja*.

Las Fallas (see page 14) on March 19th, *San José;* 2nd Sunday in May, *Día de la Virgen.* The famous statue of the Madonna, Virgen de los Desamparados, is moved from the basilica to the cathedral for a festival service. The square between the two churches is full of people when the statue is carried out and handed over to the crowd. It is passed from shoulder to shoulder, appearing to swim on a sea of people, who shout the Madonna's praises and pay her compliments. It can be a full hour before the statue arrives at the cathedral — a very impressive spectacle.

Alameda, Paseo de la Alameda 5; *Don Manuel*, Paseo de la Alameda 5; *Ateneo*, Plaza del Caudillo 18; *El Condestable*, Artes Gráficas 15; *La Hacienda*, Navarro Reverter 12; *Los Azaháres*, Navarro Reverter 16.

Les Graelles, Arquitecto Mora 2; *Gure Etxea*, Almirante Cadarso 6; *Ma Cuina*, Gran Via Germanias 49.

Oficina Municipal de Turismo in the town hall, Plaza del Caudillo; tel. 3 51 04 17.

Detail of a painting by Sorolla, Museo de Bellas Artes

Monte Picayo, on the north motorway, Puzol exit.

A special tip

A meeting of the oldest law court in Europe, the *Tribunal de las Aguas* (Water Tribunal), whose origins are lost in the first millennium, is held every Thursday morning in front of the Apostles' Doorway of the cathedral. It dispenses with lawyers, statute books and minutes — the eight elected farmers from the *huerta*, the market-garden region, settle in the Valencian language any disputes over water which their neighbours might put to them. And their decision is valid and incontestable.

Beaches of Valencia

North: By following the *Puerto* or *El Grao* signs to the harbour and turning left towards *Las Arenas*, you will come to two beaches which are most attractive. At the end of the 19th c. the people of

Valencia frequented the beaches of *Las Arenas* and *Malvarrosa*. Since then time has seemed to stand still, at least as far as architecture is concerned. In Las Arenas, the municipal swimming bath is a grandiose building with classical columns. In addition, colourfully painted changing-rooms, hot showers (*duchas calientes*) and other amenities are available for visitors returning from the beaches. Malvarrosa forms part of the *El Cabañal* fishing-quarter and is perhaps even more picturesque. Clearly, the residents of Valencia used to stroll about here, among Art Nouveau villas of every possible design, very charming bars from the same period, and elegant sanatoriums. Where the coast road turns inland, you can also carry on alongside the beach where you will come across another relic from our great-grandparents' time: wooden bathing-huts which look like garden sheds. Nowadays whole families spend their weekends here. The beach, which stretches as far as *Port Saplaya* (see page 45), is wide, beautiful and always crowded. Close to the harbour the water is not particularly clean, but the beach is delightful, and tourists hardly ever find their way here.

 Las Arenas, Playa de Levante 52; tel. 3 71 33 11. *La Carmela,* Isabel Villena 155 (Malvarrosa); tel. 3 71 00 73.

South: Drive towards El Saler on the motorway to the Pinedo exit and then take the main road to Cullera where there is a junction of the A-7 motorway with the N-332 main road to Alicante.

10 km beyond the city gates, you will see the 2-m-deep lagoon *L'Albufera* which has always been one of Valencia's landmarks. It is a fresh-water lake fed by three little rivers and has an area of 35 sq. km. A small strip of land some 1000 m wide, the *Dehesa*, separates it from the sea. Three locks (*golas*) connect the lake to the sea and enable its water-level to be controlled. It is important from an

economic point of view that the level may be raised on occasions, as it is necessary in early summer to flood the large rice-fields which surround the Albufera.

There is also something special here for the gourmet: eels, *anguilas*, and elvers, *angulas*. They are caught in nets which are suspended between posts in the lagoon.

The dense pine forests of the Dehesa merge with a wide, sandy beach. Up to now only a few places have been given over to hotels and apartment blocks. The byroads leading down to the various inviting stretches of beach are clearly signposted.

Playa Nudista: Naturist beach (turn off at the second sign).

El Saler (small seaside resort):

 La Dehesa, Playa del Saler; *Patilla*, Playa del Saler.

L'Aterrissador:

  Hotel *Sidi Saler Sol.*

L'Estany:

 Round the Albufera.

L'Alcatí (facing the sea):

 Parador *Nacional Luís Vives.*

(on the lake side):

 Dehesa Gardens: rowing boats available for trips on the Albufera.

 Also a small arena where you can try your hand at bullfighting, under close supervision.

El Palmar (turning off to the right) is a small village where some of the Albufera fishermen live. It is worth trying Valencian specialities here such as *paella, fideuá, arroz a banda,* or the Albufera dish par excellence, eel *all i pebre*, with garlic and Spanish peppers.

 Racó de l'Olla, El Lago and *El Rec.*

 Round the Albufera.

Moraira

Costa Blanca

The Costa Blanca, the 'White Coast', begins immediately beyond Valencia. Long sandy beaches stretch as far as the Cabo de San Antonio, and from here on the road passes through orange-groves broken up here and there by the market gardens of the Valencian *huerta*. Then the scenery changes; just as on the Costa Dorada, the rocks of a coastal mountain chain suddenly dip towards the sea, forming in places romantic bays which tempt the tourist. The area around Benidorm is also hilly. And why is it called the White Coast? It is the light which characterises this landscape — a bright, diffused, shimmering light, so very different from the heavier, rich tones which in northern Europe predominate on even the brightest summer day.

The route is along the N-332, the national highway, as far as Alicante, or on the A-7 toll motorway which runs parallel to it. Leave Valencia by the exit marked 'Alicante/Alacant'. Beyond Silla the road divides into the motorway and the main road. Immediately following the junction, you will see on your right the huge Ford car works of Almusafe.

Cullera AA-59

From miles away you will be able to see the huge Hollywood-type letters on the massive rock face, announcing the name of the town. But Cullera is certainly not like Hollywood. Situated on the Bahía de los Naranjos, the little town is overshadowed by an imposing hill on which can be seen the ruins of a castle and the pilgrimage church of the *Virgen del Castillo*. The once idyllic fishing village, which still has a certain charm thanks to its situation, is today a town of concrete hotel blocks for thousands of holidaymakers, mainly French. To those visitors just passing through, the climb up the hill to the castle can be recommended. From here there is an almost endless view over the plains to the Cape of San Antonio.

 A sandy beach of some 10 km extends along the coast and

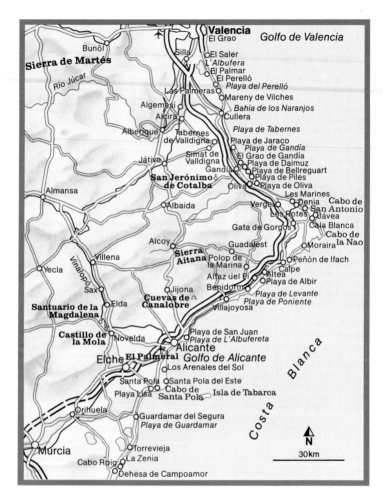

around the bays near the cape. An equally long stretch of beach may be reached by taking the coast road to the north of Cullera heading towards Valencia. Beaches to be recommended are those of *Mareny*, *Palmeras* and *Perelló*, even if the buildings are not very attractive. These beaches are frequented chiefly by Spaniards:

In Cullera:

  Swimming pool with a chute: *Tobogán Acuático*, on the beach.

  Karting Club Las Palmeras, Ctra. del Perelló.

  Club de Tenis, Ctra. del Faro.

Deportes Neptuno, Av. Cabanyal.

 Green, c. Madrid; *Tobacco Garden,* c. Agustín Oliver.

 Number One, c. Pintor Ferrer Cabrera; *New Pancho,* c. Agustín Oliver; *Triplex,* Ctra. del Faro.

⊗ *Les Mouettes,* Subida al Castillo.

✖ *Don Carlos,* Av. Castelló; *Los Olivos,* Ctra. del Faro; *Delfín,* c. Madrid; *Salvador,* Estany de Cullera.

✂ March 17th to 19th, *Fallas;* two weeks after Easter, *Virgen del Castillo.*

🎸 Every Saturday evening, concert by the local music groups in the Jardines del Mercado.

ℹ️ *Consell Municipal de Turisme,* Carrer del Riu 42; tel. (96)1 52 09 74.

🚌 To the monastery of *Simat de Valldigna* (about 25 km). Leaving Cullera on the N-332 in the direction of Gandía, turn off to Tabernes de Valldigna and then follow the signs. The royal monastery was founded in 1297 by James II of Aragón, who had it well fortified in order to protect the monks from the frequent raids by Moorish pirates. The buildings have been privately owned since the 19th c. and in 1982 extensive restoration work was begun. Inside the monastery church, the Baroque dome is a particularly impressive sight.

On the other side of the Cape of Cullera the coast consists of a very wide sandy beach which extends beyond Gandía. On the way to Gandía there are no real holiday facilities to speak of. The beach, however, is of the best quality.

 Playa de Tabernes (AA-59) has a magnificent beach and a development along two streets which is a common format in this area. Small coastal tracks lead to the undeveloped little beaches between here and Cullera.

Playa de Jaraco (Xeraco, AA-60) is an almost deserted beach.

Gandía Pop. 55,000; AA-60

Immediately on the right as you approach the town you will see the *Castillo de Bayren* fortress, which dominates the skyline. The town itself lies a short distance inland and has an important fishing harbour, *El Grao,* on the coast, close to which the well known Gandía beach stretches for miles in both directions.

🐎 The hill on which the Castillo stands was utilised by the Romans and the Arabs for strategic purposes, yet the history of the town itself does not begin until the Reconquest by the Christians in about the middle of the 13th c. As long ago as 1299 the region was raised to a duchy by the kings of Aragón. At the end of the 15th c. Pope Alexander VI, a Borgia, acquired the duchy for his family. The splendour which developed at the court of Gandía under the Borgias was matched only by that of the Italian courts of the Renaissance. Unfortunately the prosperity of the town was so closely tied to the fate of the ducal family that their decline also brought about the downfall of Gandía, turning it into a provincial backwater.

📷 Even today you can sense the atmosphere in the various buildings which date from the time of the Borgias' splendour. If you come by car, it is best to park on the *Aparcamiento Municipal* on the bank of the River Serpis below the Borgia Palace. The ancestral seat of the family, known as the *Palacio Ducal* (Ducal Palace), is an illustration of two stormy centuries in the history of the Mediterranean coast of Spain, and it demonstrates just how

Gandía

Italianised the Borgias were. It is a building of the late Gothic and early Italian Renaissance periods, severe and dignified yet with decorative details which confer on it a certain charm. In the last century the palace was sold by the Borgia heirs to the Jesuits; they make every effort to maintain it, but there is obviously a shortage of money. Visiting is only possible with a guide.

The most important rooms are as follows. The *Galería Dorada* built in 1671 is divided up by gilded stucco arches. Each section of the gallery has a different ceiling decoration, and some of the rooms contain valuable paintings. In the first room, for instance, there is a triptych by Juan de Juanes and in the second is a portrait by Jacinto Espinosa of the 10th duke, who had the gallery built. In the last room the floor is laid with a unique multicoloured mosaic made up of Manises tiles. They depict, within a circular form, the elements of creation, and were specially made for this room.

The original tiled floors are preserved in other rooms too, such as the *Sala de la Abuela* (the 'grandmother's room'), and give some idea of the former splendour of the palace. The private chapel, *Santa Capilla*, of the Jesuit Francisco Borgia (1510–72), who was canonised 100 years after his death, is also very impressive. If you disregard the vulgar 19th c. restorations which Count Rótova donated to the Jesuits, then what remains clearly demonstrates the asceticism of the man who had this place of prayer built in the shape of a coffin to remind himself of life's transience. The etchings decorating the side walls and portraying the Mysteries of the Rosary were done by his daughter Dorotea.

The road on which the Borgia palace is situated opens out onto the main square, *Plaça de la Constitució*. On one side, appearing somewhat out of place and forlorn, stands the neoclassical *town hall* (18th c.) which was never completed. On the opposite side is the 14th c. *Church of Santa María,* which was extended in the 16th c. The church's two doorways and the gargoyle on the façade overlooking the square are very fine, but unfortunately the interior was devastated by fire during the Civil War. In the modern part of the town, above the palace, you can take an evening stroll along the wide boulevard called the Passeig de les Germanies, and enjoy the lively scene.

 The huge wide sandy beach to the north and south of the harbour, El Grao, is probably one of the finest in Spain. Because of its size, it does not become too crowded even at weekends. The many restaurants along the beach are to be recommended.

    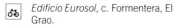

Gourmets flock to Gandía for the best dishes on the Valencian coast. Typical, and similar to paella, is *fideuá* in which noodles are used instead of rice. Restaurants: *As de Oros,* Passeig Marítim Neptú 28, El Grao; *Emilio,* Av. Vicente Calderón 5, El Grao; *La Gamba,* Ctra. Nazaret-Oliva, El Grao; *Kayuko,* c. Verge 5, El Grao; *Mesón de los Reyes,* Mallorca 47, El Grao; *Rincón de Avila,* Plaça d'Orient 4, El Grao.

El Asombro, Camino Viejo de Valencia, El Grao; *Los Sauces,* Ctra. de Daimuz, Gandía.

La Baccará, c. Legazpi, El Grao; *Flash Flash,* Colonia Ducal, El Grao; *Rompeolas,* Passeig Marítim Neptú, El Grao.

Edificio Eurosol, c. Formentera, El Grao.

Hotel *Los Robles,* c. Formentera, El Grao.

Club de Tenis, Ctra. Nazaret-Oliva, El Grao; *Poliesportiu Municipal,* Av. dels Esports, Gandía.

On the Passeig Marítim Neptú.

March 17th, *Fallas*; during Easter week processions take place; feasts of the patron saints (Miguel/ Francisco Borgia), lasting for two weeks from about September 29th/October 3rd onwards, with processions, music, dancing, etc.

i *Oficina Municipal de Turismo,* Av. Marqués de Campo s/n, tel. (96) 2 87 45 44; also Passeig Marítim Neptú s/n, El Grao, tel. (96) 2 84 24 07.

Excursions into the hinterland

San Jerónimo de Cotalba

This former monastery, 7 km on the road to Játiva/ Albaida, is situated on a flat-topped hill on the right of the road, overlooking a delightful fertile valley. It is approached through a long avenue of trees. The monastery was built in 1388 for Hieronymite monks whose original home on the coast had been raided on several occasions by pirates. Since the expropriation of church property in the 19th c., the splendid buildings have become somewhat dilapidated, but the present owners have plans for a complete restoration programme. If this goes ahead it should be possible to see again in their former glory not only the Mudéjar and Renaissance cloisters but also the beautiful chapel which contains frescos by the Valencian Nicolás Borrás. Until that time, the visitor must be content to enjoy the lush gardens and the grand avenue of trees. In the evening, especially, it is rewarding to escape from the hurly-burly of Gandía to this setting of peace and tranquillity.

In the locality generally.

Játiva (Xátiva)

The birthplace of the two Borgia popes, Calixtus and Alexander, will be particularly interesting for those who wish to trace further the history of this fascinating family. But quite apart from the Borgias, Játiva used to be one of the most important towns in the kingdom of Valencia and has much to offer the visitor.

Játiva has been inhabited since time immemorial. Even Neanderthal skulls have been found here. The Romans called this Iberian town Saetabis Augusta, and the Arabs called it Medina Xateba. Játiva's prominence began under Arab rule and lasted until 1707, when Philip V put an end to it.

In the 11th c., the very first paper to be manufactured in Europe was produced here under Abu Masaifa, and the town became a centre for arts and crafts. In 1244 James I of Aragón conquered Játiva, which soon rose to become the second town in the kingdom of Valencia. In the 15th c. the two Borgias who were to become popes were born here; unfortunately however they cared more about Gandía than they did about Játiva.

The inhabitants here were always courageous and ready to put up resistance against their foes. They paid dearly, however, for their stand against the Bourbon pretender, Philip V, in the War of the Spanish Succession at the beginning of the 18th c. Philip had this town of enthusiastic followers of the Austrian cause set on fire and the inhabitants driven out. He ordered that from thenceforth Játiva was to be called San Felipe. Although the town is called by its old name today, it has never been able to regain the greatness it once knew. For that reason the portrait of Philip V in the town's museum is incorrectly hung, so that he appears to be blushing for shame!

The Old Town lies at the foot of massive fortifications and is separated from the New Town by a shady avenue known as the Alameda. You are advised to park your car at the western end of the Alameda and enter the Old Town through the Porta San Francesco. Immediately next to this gate is the Gothic *Franciscan Monastery*, the restoration of which began in 1984. Straight up the hill towards the fortress you come to the *Museo Municipal* (Municipal Museum) which is housed in the old granary, the *Almudí*, a building dating back to the 16th c. On the ground floor archaeological finds are on display, three of which are of particular interest. First there is a 9th c. Arab water basin in pink marble and decorated with scenes from oriental everyday life, which is unique in that it blatantly violates the Muslim law against portraying any living creature; then there are the very well preserved Gothic wayside cross and the richly decorated wooden ceiling. On the upper floor there are some very good pictures by José de Ribera (known as 'Il Spagnoletto'), by Vicente López, Falcó and the Valencian Impressionist artists Benlliure, Rusiñol and Constantino Gómez, as well as the portrait of the vengeful Philip V. (Open: Monday to Friday 10 a.m.–1 p.m., 4–6 p.m; Saturday and Sunday 10 a.m.–1 p.m.)

If you now follow the Carrer de la Corretgería in a westerly direction you come to the Plaza Calixto III which is bounded by two Renaissance palaces and the cathedral. The former Dominican Monastery (*Santo Domingo/ Sant Domènec*) dating from the 15th c. stands a short distance from the square in the Calle Nevatería Vieja. It is in ruins, but is to be restored. In the square itself is the *Hospital Civil*, built in the 15th–16th c. and still in use as a hospital today. Its Italian Renaissance style is doubtless attributable to the influence of the Borgias. The magnificent façade is asymmetrical. To the left are four huge Renaissance windows and below them a small doorway in the same style. This is balanced on the right-hand side by a taller door of the late Gothic period. The patients do not appreciate sightseers in the hospital.

The *cathedral*, which took almost 400 years to build (up to 1920), stands majestically opposite the hospital. The façade, which is the latest addition, looks a little out of place. The proportions of the building are just as immense as those of the cathedral in Valencia. The high altar (1808) was designed by the Madrid architect Ventura Rodríguez, and the statue of the Madonna was created by a modern sculptor, Mariano Benlliure. In the cathedral treasury there is a 15th c. altarpiece by Jacomart, which was commissioned by Calixtus III. Of the façades, the 17th c. Baroque north front, opening on to a flight of steps, is the most attractive.

If you now go back to the Almudí and turn left, you can walk up to the *fortress*; it is a steep climb but worth it for the view alone. Just outside the town boundary at the beginning of the way up, on the left and right, are the chapels of *San José* and *San Félix (Sant Josep, Sant Feliu)*. San Félix stands on the ruins of the Visigothic cathedral in the centre of the Roman Saetabis and is one of the three surviving Romanesque churches in Valencia. Today it functions as a museum, housing magnificent altarpieces from other churches in the town which no longer exist. To the left, near the entrance, you can see a 13th c. Romanesque baptismal font with a relief portraying scenes from the Birth of Christ. The high altar is notable for its twenty-seven scenes by an unknown 15th c. master. (Open: 10 a.m –1 p.m., 3–6 p.m., except Monday.)

It is possible to walk round the *fortifications*, which date from many different periods. The neo-Gothic buildings which the owners — the fortress is in private hands — constructed during the last century are a little obtrusive, but one can nevertheless recognise even today that this was one of the most important strongholds in Spain during the late Middle Ages. If you like walking, you will certainly enjoy yourself

here. (Open: 10.30 a.m.–2 p.m., 4.30–8 p.m., except Monday.)

 Casa de la Abuela, c. Reina 17.

Feria de Agosto, August 15th to 20th. Bullfights in the Art Nouveau arena, folk-dancing and craft fairs.

Oficina Municipal de Turismo, c. Alameda Jaume I 35; tel. (96) 2 27 55 61.

Albaida

If you are interested in modern Spanish art then you should return to the coast via the little town of Albaida. This was the home of the painter José Segrelles (1886–1969) who is well known for his lively and rather impressionistic illustrations to 'Don Quixote'. His fellow citizens have devoted a museum to him, which contains a very good selection of his works (the *Museo de José Segrelles,* open 9 a.m.–1 p.m., 4–6 p.m.). The imposing *Palacio del Marqués de Albaida* and the *parish church* are both worth visiting. The palace was built in the style of a fortress with three defence towers in the main façade. The interior has been preserved in a simple Baroque style. (Enquire about opening times.)

To the south of Gandía various beaches may be reached from the main highway via little byroads. The beaches are as wide and sandy as in Gandía itself, but only rarely used by tourists. If you prefer to keep away from crowds then you will probably find exactly what you are looking for at the *Playa de Daimuz (Daimus), Playa de Guardamar, Playa de Bellreguart* or *Playa de Piles.*

Oliva AA-61

This bustling little market town has an attractive and peaceful seaside development with a wide sandy beach. A small marina was recently built here.

Pedalos.

 On the Oliva beach link road. The go-karting firm also offers flights in ultra-light gliders.

 Cavall Bernat, Ctra. de Gandía 22.

 The *Vergel Safari Park* lies between Oliva and Denia on the road which branches off inland towards Pego. It is not particularly well run, but nevertheless makes an enjoyable afternoon's outing, especially for the children. Apart from the usual animals 'in the wild', there are also South American pumas and llamas, not to mention the snake and dolphin displays.

You now cross the provincial border and head towards Alicante. You will notice a fundamental change in the scenery. The flat seashore with its long stretches of beach is replaced by the steep *Sierra de Montgó* which thrusts itself out into the sea like a hand, ending at the capes of San Antonio and de la Nao. The seaside resorts can only be reached over winding roads leading off the main road or motorway.

Denia AA-62

Denia lies in the foothills of the Sierra. The western part of the town with its harbour is dominated by the ruins of a large fortress built on top of a hill. In spite of its popularity as a tourist town, Denia has retained its original charm. It is true that it has no impressive monuments to speak of, yet it has all the characteristics of life in a small, peaceful Mediterranean town which makes a living from farming its hinterland and from fishing. The town has a long but not particularly significant history. The Greeks called it Artemision, but this was changed to Dianium by the Romans. Under the Arabs it was for a short time the capital city of a small principality, and when the Habsburgs ruled over it Denia was granted as feudal tenure to the Duke of Lerma, the

infamous favourite of Philip II. In the 19th c. English merchants settled in the town and were involved in the export of raisins. This explains the old-fashioned English company signs which are to be seen in the Old Town.

 To the west of the harbour lies the wide sandy beach of *Les Marines.* To the east, where the coastline becomes rocky, the section of the town known as *Les Rotes* has a few rocky bays.

 El Pegolí, Ctra. de les Rotes s/n; *Mesón Troya,* Ctra. de les Rotes s/n; *Casa Juan,* Ctra. Las Marinas 464.

You can visit various natural caves in the foothills of the Sierra de Montgó. The *Cova Tallá,* reached by a narrow path starting at the old watch-tower, *Torre del Gerro,* lies on the seashore. You can also reach it by boat. Very close to the watch-tower is the *Cova de l'Aigua Dolç,* a freshwater grotto which has no outlet to the sea.

A liqueur known as Carnot is distilled from twenty-one aromatic plants found in the Sierra de Montgó.

2nd week in July, *Fiesta de la Santísima Sangre de Cristo:* regattas, processions, music and 'Bous de Mar', a type of bullfight in which the bull is not killed but has to be driven into the sea. August 15th–16th, San Roque, *Moros y Cristianos;* March 17th, San José, *Fallas.*

Oficina Municipal de Turismo, c. Patricio Ferrandis s/n; tel. (96) 5 78 09 57.

If you do not wish to visit the seaside resorts around the capes of San Antonio and de la Nao, then drive south inland on the N-332 main road or the A-7 motorway. Do not miss the little town of *Gata de Gorgos* (AA-62) which is on the way, as it is one of the basket-making centres, and shops have on offer

Jávea

baskets, mats and other wickerwork at favourable prices. If you would like to explore the villages around the capes at your leisure, you should make use of the little road leading out of Denia in an easterly direction. If you have a definite destination in mind it would be better to take one of the many turnings off the N-332.

Jávea (Xábia) AA-62

The little town itself lies inland at the foot of the Montgó which is almost 800 m high. Its seaside resort, however, extends between the Cabo de San Antonio and the Cabo de la Nao, but there is only a small sandy beach here and this may be why it has been spared from mass tourism. Nevertheless, the delightful hills around Jávea are dotted with villas occupied by both foreign and Spanish holidaymakers.

Jávea itself is a sleepy little town dominated by a magnificent fortified church dating back to the 15th c. and built in the Castilian Gothic style. The tiny fishing harbour *Aduanas de Mar* lies on the Cabo de San Antonio, but the main attraction of the area is its scenery. If you like walking and enjoy a good view from wind-swept cliffs then this is the place for you.

 There are a large number of bays with stony beaches between the two capes. Good sandy beaches can be found only at the *Playa El Arenal*, by the Parador Nacional, and at the *Playa de Granadella*, a sandy bay which lies on the other side of the Cabo de la Nao.

 Pedalos.   **S**

 Playa El Arenal. *Cala Blanca.*

Parador; *Parque Calablanca,* with water-chute; *Ciudad Residencial Toscamar.*

 On the road heading out towards the Cabo de la Nao.

Club Náutico de Jávea, Aduanas de Mar.

Bowling Jávea, Playa El Arenal.

 Girasol, Ctra. de Calpe.

🎵 *Molí Blanc*, Ctra. del Cabo de la Nao; *Caracol*, Ctra. del Cabo de la Nao; *Menta Swim*, Ctra. Jávea-Benitachell.

🍸 *Mimbre*, Playa El Arenal; *La Bruja*, Montánas; *Café Trecia*, c. Andrés Lambert, Aduanas.

⊗ *Villa Selina*, Partida Puchol 96; *Tosalet Casino Club*, El Tosalet development; *Parador Nacional* (with a lovely terrace of palm trees); *Ciudad Residencial Toscamar*, Ctra. Cabo de la Nao.

✗ *Da Pietro*, Playa El Arenal (Italian); *Mesón Cristóbal Colón*, Playa El Arenal; *El Blasón*, Cristo del Mar.

🚶 Mostly on the hills of the two capes, from where the Balearic island of Ibiza can be seen on a clear day.

☷ *Club de Tenis Jávea*; Ciudad Residencial Toscamar.

✂ June 15th–24th, San Juan: *Fogueres* and *encierros*. End of August, Aduanas: *feria* with encierros.

ℹ *Oficina Municipal de Turismo*, Pl. Almirante Bastarreche 24; tel. (96) 5 79 07 36.

Moraira AA-63

There is still some charm left in Jávea, but in Moraira everything seems to have been carried to excess. Thousands of tiny villas are strewn over the lovely hills just as though a giant had scattered a sack of pebbles over the area. It is lacking in any infrastructure but, in spite of that, you can still enjoy the pleasant provincial scenery and the turquoise blue bays.

 Playa del Castillo.

 Pedalos.

El Portet, the bay which lies to the north of Moraira, is most attractive. There are a few fishermen's cottages, a tiny sandy beach, unbelievably blue water and a superb view to the south over Calpe. In addition, there is a small restaurant specialising in fish dishes.

Calpe AA-63

The townscape is characterised by the nearby rocks of the *Peñón de Ifach*, which forms a peninsula rising 328 m out of the sea. The Peñón de Ifach is by now one of the definitive landmarks of the whole Costa Blanca — and rightly so, as these rocks in the sea are a typical feature of the Mediterranean, like those at Monaco or Gibraltar. In Calpe the widely spread developments are similar to those found in Jávea and Moraira, although the town centre has retained all the characteristics of a typical Mediterranean village. On the outskirts the white villas cling to the slopes, while the beaches on both sides of the Peñón are backed by wide boulevards.

☷ *Playa de Levante* to the north of the headland is a wide sandy beach over a kilometre long with facilities for waterskiing and surfing. *Playa El Arenal* lies between headland and village and has small sandy bays. Pedalos may be hired from both beaches.

☷ *Club de Tenis*, Camino Viejo de Benisa.

☷ *Club de Tenis*, Camino Viejo de Benisa.

S Boats may be hired from the fishing harbour of Puerto Pesquero.

∪ *Club de Equitación*, Urbanización Maryvilla.

▣ *La Merced*.

Bicycles: *Rentacar Turisol*, c. Balandros. Mopeds: *Rentacar Victoria*, Av. Gabriel Miró.

Au Petit Coin de France, Playa de Levante; *Casita Suiza*, c. Jardín; *Rincón de Paco*, c. Oscar Esplá; *Baydal*, at the fishing harbour.

La Fragata Blanca, c. Pescadores; *Kentucky*, Av. Gabriel Miró.

Puerto Blanco, Urbanización La Canuta; *México*, Urbanización La Merced.

On the Peñón de Ifach.

Centro de Iniciativas Turísticas, Av. Ejércitos Españoles 40; tel. (96) 5 83 12 50.

Calpe itself extends between the Peñón de Ifach and the rocky projection of the *Morro de Toix* to the south. From this point the shoreline is very varied, consisting sometimes of rocky bays and sometimes of pebbly beaches, which finally merge into the vast sandy beaches of Benidorm.

Altea AA-64.

This well maintained village presents a distinct contrast to Benidorm. It is basically a quiet place, with a small harbour and a townscape dominated by the church situated at its highest point. The steep and narrow streets with their tiny whitewashed houses are charming. However, tourism has left its mark on Altea: many artists and craftsmen have taken up residence in the little houses and there are numerous small bars, with or without music. In short, the Bohemian world has discovered Altea without actually ruining it; fishermen and artists live in harmony next to one another. The village is thus a very popular place for an outing, especially in the evening.

The rough stony beach has helped to give Altea its special character. Do not be put off by it — some people actually prefer the shingle as it has fewer insects and no sand to get thrown about.

Pedalos. **S**

Golf Don Cayo.

Submarinismo, Av. del Puerto.

Club de Tenis, Partida de Carbonera.

Posada San Miguel, Conde de Altea 24; *Sol Playa*, Edificio Sol.

Trovador, Ctra. Valencia-Alicante; *La Notte*, c. Emilio Delgado.

Hollywood, c. Constitución; *Hierba*, c. Mare Nostrum.

Centro de Iniciativas Turísticas, Paseo Marítimo; tel. (96) 5 84 23 01.

Alfaz del Pí AA-64

This town lies to the south of Altea and consists mainly of small villa developments. A small mountain ridge, the *Sierra Helada*, begins here and runs parallel to the coast, separating Altea from Benidorm. There is a magnificent view from the Cape of Punta Bombarda over Altea and the fine pebble beach of *Playa de Albir*.

Altea

Benidorm

Benidorm AA-65

It is difficult to find words to express what has been 'achieved' here in the way of tourist development during the last twenty years. The people of Valencia do not even try; they simply call Benidorm 'Manhattan', and that is the most appropriate description.

The old town of Benidorm lay on a rocky promontory (known today for publicity purposes as the Balcón del Mediterráneo) and overlooked two completely sheltered bays. The old town has almost disappeared now, and the *Playa de Levante* and the *Playa de Poniente* have developed from the two bays and are now dominated by high-rise buildings such as you would find in any large inner city. The skyscrapers were built so quickly, with so little planning, that the town was threatened by its own development. Some years ago water was scarce and had to be rationed at the height of the tourist season. The beaches seemed to be disappearing beneath the mountains of rubbish left by the tourists. Today, however, the problems have been sorted out. There is now water, and on the beaches in the early morning a 300-strong brigade of workmen fights its way past the aerobics fanatics to clean up the sand.

It is the geographical position of the town which has made it so favourable for the tourist industry. The mountain chains which surround it on all three landward sides protect it from adverse weather conditions. Lying off the coast, looking like a piece of cheese sticking out of the sea, is the island of *Islote* or *Illa de Benidorm*.

Just how many tourists visit Benidorm each year nobody knows. Estimates range between three and four million. What does the tourist expect from a town like Benidorm and what has it to offer? Obviously no one will believe that he is actually in Spain. Apart from sunshine, the beach, a donkey-ride, a paella and Flamenco dancing, everything will seem the same as in his own country. Benidorm's streets are full of restaurants, each of them with everything from English breakfasts to fish and chips on the menu. Anything locally produced here is actually

completely artificial, sterilised in cling-film, so to speak, for the tourist. However, this Mediterranean Birmingham has its advantages. Nowhere else on the coast is there such a wide variety of tourist attractions. There is also a great deal to be said for the excitement of Benidorm's nightlife. And should you find you have had enough of that, then you can easily take a day trip into the surrounding countryside or enjoy a relaxing evening in Altea.

 Club Ultraligeros, Partida Plá de Serra; tel. 5 85 30 67.

Playa de Levante, very crowded beach of fine sand. Sailing and windsurfing facilities. Pedalos.

At the *Cableski* complex in the bay of *Playa de Poniente,* a similar beautiful sandy beach but less crowded. Windsurfing, pedalos. *Aqualand,* Partida de Bajo s/n, Sierra Helada.

  S *Club Náutico,* Paseo Colón; tel. (96) 5 85 30 67

Centro de Actividades Subacuáticas, c. Limones; *Nemrod,* c. Alfaz, La Cala.

Hotel Pelicano/Ocas, Av. Gerona; *Club Foyetes,* Estación Trenet; *Club Marina,* Playa de Albir.

El Otro Mundo de Jaime, c. Ruzafa; Bowling Centre, Av. Mediterráneo.

Rancho Cherokee, Camino Viejo de Altea.

Jai alai, the Basque ball game, very exciting to watch: *Frontón Ederfai,* at Aqualand.

Bicycles, mopeds, motor-bikes: *Easy Riders,* Av. Mediterráneo; *Beniped,* c. Estocolmo.

Golf Don Cayo, Altea; 9 holes.

Minigolf, Av. Mediterráneo.

El Cisne, Ctra. de Valencia, 4 km (with garden); *Tiffany's,* Edificio

Guadalest hill village

Guadalest scenery

Coblanca, Av. del Mediterráneo; *El Molino*, Ctra. de Valencia, 3 km; *Aitona*, c. Ruzafa 2 (grills); *Calpi*, Pl. de la Constitución (Valencian cuisine); *La Trattoria Florentina*, Av. Bilbao.

🎵 *Number One*, Ctra. Circunvalación; *Black Sunset*, c. Lepanto.

🍷 *Pachá*, Rincón de Loix; *Régine's*, Av. Alcoy; *Bonny*, c. Lepanto; *New Look*, Av. Alcoy; *Benidorm Palace*, Av. Diputación, Rincón de Loix (shows, music).

🎰 *Casino Costa Blanca*, on the N-332, towards Villajoyosa.

ℹ️ *Oficina Municipal de Turismo*, c. Martínez Alejos 16; tel. (96) 5 85 32 24; *Centro de Iniciativas Turísticas*, Av. Almendros 5, tel. (96) 5 85 69 86.

🚌 ## Excursion to the hill village of Guadalest (27 km)

Take the C-3318 to Polop de la Marina and from there keep straight on to Guadalest. You soon come to the hills of the *Sierra Aitana*, which lie behind Benidorm and from where you can enjoy a spectacular view over the coast. The village of Guadalest, set on a huge rocky promontory, lies within the old fortifications which are now largely in ruins. It is tiny, with just one street and little whitewashed houses. Many buildings butt up against the rock or are half built into it, as for example is the church tower, beneath which a lockable gate in the rock gives access to the village.

Two small museums give the village an added charm — the *Museo Ribera Girona*, a modern art museum on the way to the village gate, and the unique *El Mundo de Max* (Max's World), which is close to the large car park at the entrance to the village. This museum was founded by a Spanish hypnotist who enjoyed a certain fame in America. He collected miniatures which are now on display here: stuffed fleas, matchstick sculptures, and paintings done on pinheads. Magnifying glasses are provided!

As Guadalest is promoted by every travel agent it is probably best not to come here at the weekend, when the village becomes so crowded you can hardly move.

Villajoyosa (La Vila Joiosa) AA-66

Like Altea, Villajoyosa is completely different from Benidorm. The little town lies at the mouth of the Río Amadorio, which is practically always dry. Picturesque but somewhat dilapidated houses stand on its banks. In contrast to the inhabitants of other villages on these coasts, the *Vileros*, as the local people are called, are not content with just whitewashing their houses; everywhere you will see blue, red, purple and yellow, all reminiscent of the Aegean. An attractive promenade lined with palms extends behind the beach as far as the fishing harbour. All in all, this is a place which has not been deprived of its originality by tourism, and is well worth visiting.

🚤 🍴 *El Brasero*, Av. del Puerto.

🎭 The *Moros y Cristianos* of Villajoyosa from July 24th–31st is well worth seeing. The 'Moors' attack from the sea and are then driven back into it. Afterwards, there is a big procession in honour of the patron saint, St Marta. *Nardo*, a pretty explosive mixture of iced coffee and absinthe, is drunk during this festival.

ℹ️ *Centro de Iniciativas Turísticas*, Pl. Castelar 1; tel. (96) 5 89 30 43.

On the way to Alicante you can make a detour to the natural caves of *Canalobre* (branch off the N-332 18 km south of Villajoyosa). You will find the caves, which are very well lit and a very popular tourist attraction, on the slopes of the Cabeçó d'Or Mountain. Their name,

literally meaning Candelabra Caves, is explained by the shapes of the stalagmites. (Open: 11 a.m.–5 p.m.)

Alicante (Alacant) Pop. 235,000

The provincial capital lies at the northern end of a huge bay which stretches from the Cabo de Huertas to the Cabo de Santa Pola. It is dominated by the defences of the Castillo Santa Bárbara, set on the rocky slope of the Benacantil.

🔯 Alicante was first settled by the Iberians and became a trading centre under the Greeks, who called it Akra Leuke (White Mountain), and the Romans, who named it Lucentum. In 1244 the Arab Al-Lekant was conquered by Alfonso the Wise of Castile, but later, like the rest of the Valencian region, it came under the rule of Aragón. The town did not become important until the 16th and 17th c., at the time of the Spanish wars with France over ascendancy in Oran (present-day Algeria). It developed into a large naval port for the North African expeditions, but trade with these regions also flourished. About the middle of the 19th c., when Alicante was connected by a railway with Madrid, the commercial importance of the town increased.

📷 The oldest part of the town, known as *Barrios Altos*, has many picturesque little corners in the steep streets which cling to the Benacantil. However, the more significant buildings are situated further down, and date from a time when the town was expanding and people preferred the level ground to the slopes.

It is best to begin sightseeing directly below the Castillo Santa Bárbara, just before the start of the seafront promenade, *Paseo Marítimo*, which is planted with palm trees. Here, in the Calle Jorge Juan, you first come to the church of *Santa María* on your right. The present building dates mostly from the 18th c., although earlier churches stood

Alicante

on this site, and a thousand years ago there was even a mosque. The Baroque main façade of the present church was designed in 1721 by the local artist Manuel Violat. Inside there is a magnificent Baroque high altar surrounded by a grille.

The Baroque *Casa de la Asegurada* palace lies diagonally behind the church in the Plaza de Santa María. Since 1977 the municipal collection of modern art has been housed here in the *Museo Municipal de Arte del Siglo XX*. You will find works by internationally renowned artists such as Calder, Miró, Gris, Tàpies, Bacon, Braque, Picasso, Zobel de Ayala and Kandinsky. (Open: weekdays 10.30 a.m.–1.30 p.m., 6–9 p.m.; public holidays 6–9 p.m.; closed on Mondays.)

In the same street as the church of Santa María you will find the most important municipal building, the *Ayuntamiento* (town hall); of particular interest is the Baroque façade designed by Chápuli. Inside, have a look at the *chapel* which is floored with colourful tiles from Manises.

If you now turn right beyond the town hall and go along the Calle San Nicolás, you will come to the *cathedral*, dedicated to St Nicholas of Bari. The building dates from the early 17th c. and is in the austere Renaissance style which was so popular in Spain at that time. It is often referred to as the 'Escorial style' after the monastery near Madrid which Philip II built in the same

manner. The majestic interior reflects the same architectural ideas, which were symbolic of power and also asceticism. The 18th c. Baroque *communion chapel* offers an interesting contrast. The cloisters are planted with orange-trees. Nearby in the square you can watch craftsmen at work.

There is a fine panoramic view of the whole town from the Castillo de Santa Bárbara. It is easy to reach — opposite El Postiguet beach, where the tour began, there is a lift which will take you up to the Castillo.

The beaches of Alicante are all of the finest sand. The town beach *Playa del Postiguet* lies directly below the Castillo, where the Calle Jorge Juan meets the esplanade. It must be very pleasant for an Alicantino to go there for a swim at the end of the working day, and it gets very full at this time. *Playa de l'Albufereta*, 3 km from the town centre and sheltered by the Cabo de Huertas, is very built up and is equally popular. You can also swim in the coves of the rocky *Cabo de Huertas*, where there are several apartment blocks. *Playa de San Juan* is today a seaside resort whose size reminds you of Benidorm. Yet the golden sandy beach stretches for more than 10 km so there is no lack of space.

Delfín, Explanada de España 14 (fish dishes and various sorts of paella); *La Piel del Oso,* Urbanización Vistahermosa (international cuisine); *El Jumillano,* c. César Elguezábal 62 (Alicante cuisine); *Pizzería Romana,* Finca Las Palmeras, La Albufereta (French and Italian). *Nou Manolín,* c. Villegas 3; *La Côte du Boeuf,* Ctra. de Alcoy, 7 km (with garden); *La Dársena,* Club Náutico, Muelle Costa (at the harbour).

Golf Peñas Rojas, Ctra. de Castalla, 15 km (18 holes); Playa de San Juan: *Club de Golf Amaina Park* (36 holes).

June 21st–24th, *Hogueras de San Juan*; similar to the Valencian Fallas but of more recent origin.

ℹ️ *Oficina Regional de Turismo*, Explanada de España 2; tel. (96) 5 21 22 85. *Centro de Iniciativas Turísticas*, c. Portugal 17; tel. (96) 5 22 38 02.

🚌 Excursions into the hinterland

To Jijona (Xixona) (25 km)

This town offers the visitor no monuments and no festivals but only a traditional Spanish gourmet speciality — *turrón* (in Valencian, *terró*). This delicious type of nougat, which in contrast to the nougat of southern France is hard, is as much a part of Spanish Christmas festivities as the Christmas tree is of our own. The Arabs are believed to have made it, and then under the Habsburgs the *jijonencos* travelled the whole of Spain as itinerant salesmen promoting this popular product.

You should visit a factory and sample it for yourself. If you develop a craving for the nougat (which is more than likely) then take as much as you can home with you, as it is virtually impossible to come by elsewhere. In the Fábrica El Lobo there is a museum where you can learn about the manufacturing process. (Open: daily 9 a.m.–1.30 p.m.)

🚌 Via Novelda and Sax to Villena (65 km)

The little towns on the way to Villena lie in a wine-producing region where the sand-coloured barren landscape is in stark contrast to the orange-groves on the coast. The bareness of this area suits a more ascetic, more frugal breed of men than is found on the fertile east coast.

Novelda. You reach this small industrial town with its magnificent fortress by turning left 6 km beyond the 300-m-high Portichol Pass. Many different branches of industry are carried on here, including marble-quarrying, shoe manufacture and textile production. In addition, the majority of the saffron produced in Spain is packaged in Novelda. In short, the place typifies the proverbially hard-working character of Alicante province.

3 km from the town is the *Castillo de la Molaf*, set on a hill overlooking the Vinalopó River. The fortress is of Arab origin and was besieged and burnt by El Cid. The two towers and the masonry are very well preserved. One of the 15th c. towers is triangular in form — a technical rarity. Close to the fortress stands the pilgrimage church *Santuario de la Magdalena*. It was designed by the local architect José Sala y Sala (1908), who was inspired by the work of the genius from Barcelona, Antoní Gaudí. A feature of the building is the uneven masonry laid with tiles. If you are interested in this particular style then you should also visit the *Museo Modernista*, c. Mayor 22, Novelda. (Open: weekdays, 11 a.m.–2 p.m., 7–9.30 p.m.)

Above **Sax** towers a steep rocky mound on top of which is the fortress of the same name, which has retained the form of its Moorish construction. Anyone who has the energy to climb up to it will be rewarded with a spectacular view over the plain. A museum has been constructed within the walls with a display of national costumes and an explanation of the festival of Moros y Cristianos. (Open: Saturday 5–8 p.m.; Sunday noon–2 p.m., 5–8 p.m. If it is closed the key can be obtained from the town hall.)

🍴 *El Molino*, Ctra. de Salinas (swimming pool).

Villena is recognised from a distance by the imposing silhouette of the *Castillo de la Atalaya*, the former seat of the Marqués de Villena.

After its reconquest in the 13th c. Villena was an important Castilian border fortress confronting the people of Aragón. In the 15th c. the notorious Marqués Enrique de Villena lived here; on the one hand, to his great credit, he translated Virgil and Dante into Spanish, but on the other hand he dabbled in black magic. He was succeeded as Marqués by the elder of the infamous Pacheco brothers who was the favourite of Henry IV of Castile. First he robbed the king of half his fortune, then he forced him to promise his sister, Isabella of Castile, in marriage to his brother Pedro Pacheco. Isabella, who not without reason was later known as 'Her Catholic Majesty', prayed and fasted in her desperation, until Pedro, who was due to come and fetch her, unexpectedly died from diphtheria only one day's ride away.

 The fortress with its double ring of walls is one of the best-preserved in the whole of Valencia. In view of the way it was built this is not surprising: the walls of the main tower are a good 3 m thick. There are also some halls extant, with Moorish domes. The *Church of Santiago* in the town is notable for the splendid twisted columns in its Gothic interior.

Villena is best known today, however, for its treasure (*Tesoro de Villena*), which was discovered in 1963 and is displayed in the *Ayuntamiento* (town hall), a Baroque palace with some Renaissance features. The treasure dates from the Bronze Age and consists of more than sixty pieces (vessels, utensils, etc.) of pure gold. It is the largest treasure of this kind in Europe and is fascinating because of the simple designs which are somewhat reminiscent of African art.

Leaving the industrial region to the south of Alicante and heading along the coast towards the Cabo de Santa Pola, you will find vast sandy beaches, which around *Arenales del Sol* cater for tourists. The best of all, however, are those extensive undeveloped stretches where you can have the whole of the seashore to yourself.

Santa Pola

As well as having long sandy beaches, Santa Pola is one of the most important fishing ports on the Mediterranean coast of Spain, so tourism is somewhat neglected. Most of its visitors are Spaniards who are content with the modest facilities. There is nothing of any real interest in the town; only a few walls of the old fortress are still standing and these house the municipal library.

 To be recommended are the *Gran Playa* and the *Playa Lisa*, which are to the west of the harbour, and the *Playa de Levante* to the east. Also to the east is the beach of *Santa Pola del Este*, a seaside holiday development.

 Pedalos.

  Gran Playa; Santa Pola del Este; Polideportivo Municipal, Av. Valencia.

 Gran Playa; Santa Pola del Este.

Near the cemetery (*Cementerio*).

S *Club Náutico* at the harbour.

U *Gran Playa.*

Santa Pola del Este.

Santa Pola has an excellent reputation for its culinary delights, especially seafood, for example at the *Batiste,* near the harbour. *Mesón del Puerto,* c. Fernando Pérez Ojeda 2; *Gaspar's,* Playa de Levante; *Miramar,* at the harbour.

Muelle II, c. del Muelle.

♫ *Concord,* c. Marqués de Molins; *Much More,* Cruce de la Sentanera.

🚌 **Excursions to the island of Nueva Tabarca and the hinterland.**

Nueva Tabarca is 3 miles off the coast and can be reached by boat. In previous centuries this flat island was a favourite base for pirates from North Africa. In 1770 the island was occupied by Genoese who had been imprisoned on an island of the same name off Tunis, and who had been ransomed by the Spanish king. The impressive fortifications serve as a reminder of those times. The village called San Pablo is a fishing community, picturesque in parts but rather run down in others where the keen salty wind has destroyed the plaster on the houses. There are sandy beaches and bays where small beach restaurants serve paellas and fish dishes.

ℹ *Centro de Iniciativas Turísticas,* Pl. Diputación s/n; tel. (96) 5 41 49 84.

Elche (Elx) Pop. 190,000

This town is situated on the C-3317, 13 km beyond Santa Pola. Although Elche has only a few monuments it is one of the best-known towns in Spain. The date-palm forest which encircles it is the largest in the whole of Europe. *El Palmeral* is divided up into several *huertos* (gardens), and is not only scenic but serves economic and even religious purposes. As in Arab countries, the harvest is gathered in winter when workers climb the trees and pick the dates by hand. In some huertos lemon, fig and other fruit trees are planted among the palms. No town in Spain is without palm fronds from Elche on Palm Sunday. The most interesting huerto, in which you can walk among the palm trees, is the *Huerto del Cura* (follow the signposts). Among other things there is a

Date palms at Elche

unique 'Imperial Palm' with a sevenfold trunk. (The Palmera Imperial may be viewed from 9 a.m.–8 p.m.)

In the town itself, a visit to the area around the church of *Santa María* is worth while. The massive Baroque sandstone building dates from the 17th–18th c. and is crowned by a typically Valencian blue glazed dome. The marble high altar was designed by the church architect Jaime Bort and was made in Naples. There is a superb view over the Palmeral from the tower. The church is best known for the mystery play *El Misterio de Elche* (*Misteri d'Elx*) which is performed here in August. Mystery plays were very popular in the Middle Ages until the Tridentine Council of 1545 forbade such performances in churches. An exception was made in the case of Elche. This is therefore the oldest and at the same time the most authentic mystery play in the world. The original 13th c. text was written in French Limousin dialect or an early form of Valencian. The music dates from the 16th c. The mystery play tells of the

Orihuela

Orihuela

Orihuela lies 32 km beyond Elche on the N-340. This enchanting town nestles between its huge treeless mountain La Muela, the River Segura and a little palm grove. What makes Orihuela such an interesting place is its atmosphere — that of a proud Spanish provincial capital in the heart of the country. Two great modern-day Spanish authors gained inspiration here: José Martínez Ruiz, known as Azorín (1873–1967), and Gabriel Miró (1879–1930), who described the town in detail in his novels but referred to it as Oleza. In addition the well known poet Miguel Hernández (1910–42) hailed from Orihuela.

death and assumption into heaven of the Virgin, and is performed from August 11th–15th.

From the basilica it is just a step to the Plaza del Palacio on the banks of the River Vinalopó. Standing in this square is the *Palacio de Altamira,* a 15th c. fortified palace with walls dating from Arab times. There are more palms growing along the river-bank in the *Parque Municipal* (municipal park). The *Museo Arqueológico Municipal* is in the park, and on display here are important finds from excavations made at Elche. It was here that the *Dama de Elche* was found — the world-famous bust of a woman which dates from the Iberian period (approximately 4th c. B.C.). The strong Greek influence is shown in her head-dress. In the museum, however, only a replica of the bust is to be seen as the original is in Madrid.

The first definite references to the town go back to the time of the Visigoths when Aurariola ('pot of gold') was a provincial capital. When the Arabs wished to occupy the town in 713, the clever Gothic governor Theodomir succeeded in establishing Orihuela and its province as a Christian kingdom paying tribute to the Moors. This state of affairs, found nowhere else in the whole of the peninsula, lasted for almost a century after which Orihuela fell under Muslim rule until 1264, when the town was captured by James I of Aragón. In 1564 it became a cathedral city and was granted a university thanks to Fernando de Loaces, Archbishop of Valencia and a native of Orihuela. In the War of the Spanish Succession the town supported the Austrian Archduke Charles, was captured by the enemy and sustained heavy damage. Today Orihuela is the centre of an important agricultural region, the *Vega del Segura,* whose vast plain is irrigated by the River Segura and is second only to that of Murcia in generating wealth.

The Old Town lies in the shadow of a huge massif called *La Muela,* and is bordered on the other side by the River Segura. Motorists are advised to park near the town hall either on the

Els Capellans, Huerto del Cura; *Parque Municipal,* Parque Municipal; *La Masia de Chencho,* Ctra. de Alicante.

Oficina Municipal de Turismo, Parque Municipal; tel. (96) 5 45 27 47.

Plaza Santiago or on the Plaza Condesa de Vía-Manuel. The *Ayuntamiento* (town hall) occupies a Baroque mansion, and it is worth having a look through the entrance at the fine staircase surmounted by a domed ceiling with frescos.

Opposite stands the interesting church of *Santas Justa y Rufina*, the patron saints of the town. The tower dates from the 14th c. and is square, which is unusual in this region where eight-sided towers are the norm. The works of the clock (1329) are reputed to be the oldest in Spain. The 18th c. Baroque-classical main façade forms a strong contrast to the rest of the building. The money ran out while it was being built and it is only half as high as it should have been, so that it looks strangely truncated. The interior of the church is not very interesting as it was gutted in the Civil War.

If you go down the Calle Santa Justa you come to the Plaza Condesa de Vía-Manuel, one side of which is occupied by the fine, albeit somewhat dilapidated, *Palacio del Conde de la Granja*. The palace has a handsome Baroque entrance with a staircase decorated with 18th c. Valencian painted tiles. You should also have a look at the courtyard. Behind a side entrance is a small garden café with an art gallery.

Continuing along the Calle Santa Justa you reach the small 14th c. *cathedral* with its Gothic and Renaissance doorways. The adjoining Romanesque cloisters originally belonged to a monastery which was demolished. The tower also dates from the Romanesque period. The magnificent twisted Gothic columns inside the cathedral are somewhat reminiscent of those in the church at neighbouring Villena. The side chapels are decorated with works by well known Valencian painters and sculptors; a picture of St Catharina of Monzó is of particular interest. The grilles around the choir, the high altar and the communion chapel should not be missed. In this chapel, which dates from the Renaissance, can be seen the coat of arms of Charles V.

The cloisters give access to the *Museo Diocesano* where the cathedral treasures and works by Osona and Ribera can be seen. Also on display is the famous 'Temptation of St Thomas Aquinas' by Velázquez. Near the cathedral, in the former church of *La Merced*, is an exhibition of procession groups including 'La Diablesa' (the She-Devil) which represents the triumph of the Cross over Evil. The devil is portrayed as a lecherous, horned, naked old woman and the whole work, by Nicolás Bussi, is clear evidence of the place of fantasy in medieval art.

Following the main axis of the town you see on the left the pretty *Plaza de Santa Lucía* with its mansions. Then you reach the huge *Convento de Santo Domingo*, a former Dominican monastery founded in 1550 by the town's benefactor, Archbishop Fernando de Loaces. The architect was the famous Joan Anglés who also designed the Dominican monastery in Tortosa. The university set up in the monastery existed until the expropriation of church property during the last century; now it is occupied by a

Cathedral cloisters, Orihuela

school. The monastery has a long façade in the austere Escorial style. It ends just in front of a magnificent Renaissance town gate decorated with reliefs of St Michael above the Valencian coat of arms. Inside the monastery (ask the caretaker to let you in) you will see two cloisters or courtyards adjacent to one another. Also ask the caretaker's permission (offer him a tip!) to see the refectory. Although it has been completely modernised, there is still on one of its walls a wonderful decoration made from painted glazed tiles; it dates from the 18th c. and depicts hunting scenes. The dome of the monastery chapel, which was rebuilt in the 18th c., is painted with colourful frescos. Particularly worth seeing is a Baroque altarpiece by the Valencian painter Juan de Juanes which stands in the side chapel to the left of the high altar.

On the way back to the town hall you should have a look at the *Santiago* church (15th–17th c.) which is quite close. It was here that Ferdinand and Isabella summoned the Valencian parliament in 1488. This event is commemorated by their joint coat of arms displayed on the handsome Gothic doorway. The statue of Santiago (St James) in the doorway is modern. The interior of the church is magnificent and you should make a point of seeing the group of the Holy Family by the famous sculptor Salzillo who came from Murcia.

An extensive view over plain and sea, and as far as Murcia, can be enjoyed from *La Muela*, the mountain above the town. Here stands the *San Miguel Seminary* for the training of priests. The seminary building itself dates from the 18th c. and its low but spread-out form is reminiscent of the earthquake-resistant Spanish colonial architecture in America.

⚔ *Casa Corro*, Palmeral de San Antón (situated in the small palm grove of Orihuela).

🍷 *Juan de Juanes*, Pl. Condesa Vía-Manuel 1.

ℹ️ *Oficina Municipal de Turismo*, Palacio Marqués de Ruvalcaba; tel. (96) 5 30 27 47.

When you return to the coast you can either go back through Elche or, if you found that road too busy, you can drive direct from Orihuela following the River Segura to Guardamar, which lies to the south of Santa Pola.

Guardamar del Segura

This small town is not in itself of any great interest as it was completely destroyed by an earthquake at the beginning of the last century and has been rebuilt. It does, however, lie in a most attractive part of the country. On the landward side the fertile fields are irrigated by the Segura, on whose estuary the town of Guardamar is situated. All along the seaward side extend pine, eucalyptus and palm groves, endeavouring to stop the sand dunes from encroaching on to the roads. In the distance, you can see the silhouette of a small sierra which seems to watch over this romantic scenery. With its lovely dunes this is an ideal place for long, lazy days on the beach. If you are looking for something a little more ambitious, then Santa Pola to the north and Torrevieja to the south are not far away.

Guardamar del Segura

Torrevieja

The approach to Torrevieja is marked by a particularly unattractive development which, however, has a good beach. After that there is a stretch of rocky coast and then the town itself. *'Blanca de sal, morena de soles'* ('salt-white and sun-brown'), Torrevieja makes a living from the vast salt-works situated a little further inland and which, with an area of 30 sq. km, are among the largest in Europe. The fishing industry is also very profitable. Tourism has only recently become important, so the visitor here can still enjoy the experience of everyday life in a small Spanish town. You can take an evening stroll along the charming esplanade, watch the fish auction at about 6.30 p.m. at the neat little fishing harbour, and eat in one of the very good fish restaurants.

 To the north of the town: *Playas del Cura, de los Locos* and *de la Mata.*

  Pedalos.

 Pescador, Av. Gregorio Marañón; *Miramar,* Paseo Vista Alegre 6; *Los Manueles,* Paseo Juan Aparicio.

 Xalambó, Pachá, Jet-Set.

 Pub Sevilla, Trafos, Bésame Mucho.

 Club de Golf Villamartín, near Cabo Roig (18 holes).

 Several courts.

 Go-Kart, Ctra. de Cartagena.

 To the salt-works. You can obtain the visiting times from the Tourist Information Office.

Typical of Torrevieja are sculptures made from salt.

Mid-August: *Certamen Nacional de Habaneras* (the national habanera competition). Habaneras are literally 'ladies from Havana'. The songs are those traditionally sung by the mariners of Torrevieja who took salt to Cuba in the 18th c. In July and August there are a number of gala performances of Spanish music.

[i] *Centro de Iniciativas Turísticas,* Av. Libertad 10; tel. (96) 5 71 07 22.

To the south of Torrevieja there are three more developments next to each other which still belong to the Costa Blanca and are well worth a visit: La Zenia, Cabo Roig and Dehesa de Campoamor.

La Zenia consists of well maintained bungalows and a hotel on the seafront. The coast in this area is quite rocky but there are some sandy bays.

Dehesa de Campoamor is very peaceful, and has a small marina and a pretty beach.

 Cabo Roig, Ctra. de Cartagena; Cabo Roig is considered one of the best on the coast. Speciality: fish.

 At *Club de Golf Villamartín,* near Cabo Roig (18 holes).

 Xairó, Campoamor.

Urbanización La Zenia.

Go-Kart, Ctra. de Cartagena, La Zenia.

A special tip

There is a *casino* on the esplanade in Torrevieja which is not a gambling-house but a respectable meeting-place of local high society. The saloons of the private club built in 1868 are fitted out with the best in vulgar Victoriana, some of it pseudo-Rococo and some pseudo-Moorish. If you are respectably dressed you will not be refused entry to the rooms downstairs where you can take coffee and cakes among the señores and señoras of Torrevieja.

Daybreak on the Costa Cálida

Costa Cálida and Murcia

In some respects the provincial border between Alicante and Murcia signifies a line of demarcation, for Castilian is spoken in the autonomous region of Murcia, which consists of only one province. It is here that the Costa Blanca comes to an end and is succeeded by the Costa Cálida, the 'Warm Coast'. The Murcian coastline is dominated in the north by the vast *Mar Menor* ('Lesser Sea'). With an area of 180 sq. km this is by far the largest lagoon in the whole of Spain, and its charm is derived from the long stretch of land which divides it from the sea. This strip, known as *La Manga* (the sleeve) has beaches on both sides, and although it developed far too quickly, it has a very good tourist infrastructure. On the undeveloped rocky coast beyond the Cabo de Palos and all around the naval base of Cartagena there are important mining regions, which however have seen better days. From Cartagena a little road continues, meeting the coast from time to time. Here you will find sleepy little fishing villages, some of which cater for tourists.

If you want to spend your holiday on the Costa Cálida it is as well to have a car at your disposal and not be afraid of exploring on your own.

Murcia Pop. 280,000

Murcia, the capital town of the region of the same name, lies in the centre of one of the most productive areas of Spain. The fertile plains of the River Segura, which flows through the town, produce the greater part of the Spanish lemon crop and also provide many of the vegetables the country needs.

The Murcians' agricultural success is envied by other Spaniards, but that may be partly due to the fact that the Murcians themselves rather begrudge being classed as Spaniards. They have always represented an exception. When the Arabs overran Spain in 711 the Visigothic governor, Theodomir, succeeded in retaining his province as a Christian kingdom under Moorish rule. This unique status lasted for almost a century. The town of Murcia itself was founded during the subsequent period of direct Arab rule, in the 10th c. In 1266 the territory surrendered to the kings of Castile, but still maintained a certain, if sometimes only a notional, independence from the Castilian crown. That is why today, within the framework of the constitution of 1978, Murcia still forms an independent regional entity.

The capital of the Murcians is really very rural; the normal atmosphere of a large town does not come through at all. Three eminent 18th c. men have left their mark on the town. Bishop Belluga was responsible for the magnificent Baroque façade of the cathedral, but was also a great military strategist. In the War of the Spanish Succession he held Murcia for the Bourbons by having the region flooded to defend it against the Austrian Archduke Charles. Count Floridablanca, one of the great ministers of the Enlightenment under Charles III, safeguarded the agricultural wealth of Murcia right up to the present time. Using the latest discoveries in technology he had the River Segura, the lifeline of the huerta, canalised, and constructed a network of reservoirs. The third genius from Murcia is the sculptor Francisco Salzillo or Zarzillo (1707–83) who epitomises the provincial, faintly eccentric talents of this region which developed a Baroque style all of its own. About 1800 works, of an exclusively religious nature, are attributed to him; all of them are set in a Murcian context, and the finest are on display in the *Museo de Salzillo*, where they form one of the finest collections of religious sculpture in Europe.

It will take a good half day to go round the town, but do leave sufficient time for the Salzillo figures.

Murcia with the cathedral in the foreground

You should also sample the Murcian cuisine which is famous throughout Spain. If you come by car, you will find parking space along the northern bank of the River Segura. On this boulevard there are various representative buildings of the regional and municipal governments. Close to the Ayuntamiento (town hall), bear away from the river towards the town and you immediately come to the Plaza Cardenal Belluga with the cathedral and Palacio Episcopal (bishop's residence).

The cathedral dates from the 14th–15th c. and is dominated by its mighty Baroque façade, which was created in the middle of the 18th c. and has the unusual shape of a reredos. Although the façade is decorated with various fairly small statues of saints you will look in vain for the large figure which should be on this massive 'altarpiece'. In its place are a large window and the main doorway. The relatively bright interior is Gothic and is best known for the magnificence of the side chapels. Many of them have altars and busts of saints by the famous Salzillo (*Capilla de los Vélez, Capilla de San Andrés*). The cathedral treasury *(Museo de la Catedral)* is also worth seeing. It contains various late Gothic altarpieces,

a statue of St Jerome by Salzillo and pictures by the Murcian pupil of Velázquez Villacis (1616–94), as well as by other artists of east-coast Spain, including Pedro Orrente. (Open daily: 10 a.m.–noon, 5.30–7 p.m.) From the top of the *cathedral tower* there is a superb view over the Murcian huerta and the surrounding mountain chains.

The Museo de Salzillo, the town's main attraction, is situated in the Plaza San Agustín, which you reach by following the riverside walk upstream. Branch off away from the river near the Glorieta de España and go straight up the Avenida Juan de Cierva. The museum is actually an annex of the *Ermita de Jesús* church in which the most important exhibits are on display. In addition to the fascinating studies which Salzillo carved as designs for his busts, the rooms of the museum also contain the unique Salzillo crib. In the style of the Neapolitan cribs it consists of over 500 hand-size figures and tells almost the whole history of Creation, and that of the Holy Family from the Annunciation to the Flight into Egypt. The individual figures are carved and painted in incredibly accurate detail, and in their local costume they provide an exact picture of what Murcians looked like in the 18th c. As with all Salzillo's works, the crib was partly carried out with the help of friends and pupils; some scenes are by Roque López, his principal pupil. In the case of the large figures in the museum, Salzillo's brother Juan Antonio prepared the wood for them, and his sister Inés and brother Patricio made the statues' very expressive eyes out of eggshells.

The church itself is circular and inside is surrounded on all sides by 'boxes' in which stand Salzillo's famous Holy Week procession groups. These groups (*Pasos*) are practically life size and contain up to 13 figures, some of which are wearing wigs and are accurately dressed. The most splendid Pasos are those of the Last Supper, the Kiss of Judas and the Arrest, the Scourging and the Prayer in the Garden of Gethsemane. (Open: weekdays 9.30 a.m.–1 p.m., 4–7 p.m.; Sundays and public holidays 10 a.m.–1 p.m. Closed Maundy Thursday and Good Friday.)

The Museo Internacional de Traje Folklórico, a tiny museum of national costume, is not far from the Salzillo Museum (Calle Acisclo Diaz 8). It is housed in a 16th c. seminary building which has an attractive two-storeyed courtyard. On view are costumes from all the Spanish-speaking countries as well as from other countries of the world. (Open: 10 a.m–1.30 p.m., 5–8 p.m., closed Saturdays and public holidays.)

San Miguel stands opposite the museum. This Baroque church (1666) is balanced in design and has a magnificent high altar and a statue of St Michael carved by Salzillo's pupil Roque López.

In the **Casino** (Calle Trapería), which is not really a gambling-den but, as in the majority of towns, a club for the élite, the Victorian worthies allowed their imagination to run riot. In one and the same building they installed a Pompeian and an Arab inner courtyard, and rounded the whole thing off with a ballroom in the style of Louis XV.

The Museo de Bellas Artes (Calle Obispo Frutos 12) contains chiefly works by painters from the province of Murcia, from the 16th c. to the present day, including Nicolás Villacis (17th c), a pupil of Velázquez, Germán Hernández (19th c.) and the contemporary artist Pedro Flores. Better-known names in Spanish art are also represented here: Ribera, Madrazo, the Impressionists Muñoz Degrain and Sorolla, and Picasso. (Open: Tuesday to Friday 10 a.m.–2 p.m., 5–7 p.m., Saturday and Sunday 11 a.m.– 2 p.m.; July and August, Monday to Saturday 9 a.m.–2 p.m.)

In the evening a walk along the *Paseo*

Murcia Cathedral

Malecón can be very pleasant. It is up above the Segura, bordered by cypress groves, and leads out on to the huerta. It is where the whole of Murcia traditionally gathers at sunset for an evening stroll.

⊗ *El Rincón de Pepe*, c. Sancho 1; *Hispano*, c. Lucas 7; *Los Apóstoles*, Pl. de los Apóstoles.

✕ *Alfonso X*, c. Alfonso X 6; *Asador de Castilla*, c. Peligros s/n; *Churra*, c. Marqués de los Vélez 12; *La Huertanica*, c. Infante 5.

In the Museo de Salzillo

[⚒] Holy Week: Processions with the famous Pasos by Salzillo, considered by connoisseurs the most moving Holy Week celebrations in Spain. Easter Week: *Fiesta de Primavera* (Spring Festival) is celebrated by the huerta farmers with singing, dancing, bullfighting and the 'Entierro de la Sardina' (Funeral of the Sardine), the ritual burning of a gigantic model sardine which represents the hunger of Lent. May 10th: Pilgrimage to the *Santuario de Fuensanta* outside the town. 1st half of September: *Feria* – bullfights.

[i] *Oficina de Turismo*, c. Alejandro Séiquer 4; tel. (968) 21 37 16 and 24 69 00.

San Pedro del Pinatar

The first place on this stretch of coast lies somewhat inland from the northern tip of the Mar Menor but has a fishing harbour on the Mediterranean itself. The strip of land called La Manga which separates the Mar Menor from the Mediterranean begins at this point, but it is covered with salt pans and not accessible by car from this northern end.

[⌖] *Playa de Mojón* lies on the Mediterranean to the north of the fishing harbour.

[⚒] July 16th, *Virgen del Carmen*: fishermen's pilgrimage. The Carmen Virgin is taken out to sea in fishing-boats and her praises are sung.

Santiago de la Ribera

This pretty seaside resort is reached via the suburbs of San Pedro, La Puntica and Lo Pagán. It is very Victorian, with little walkways leading out into the Mar Menor, and restaurants on the piers. Young men in Air Force uniforms can be seen everywhere as this is a military zone. The Spanish Air Force Academy is situated here as is one of the largest

bases, San Javier; its runways occupy the Mar Menor beach to the south of Santiago. For this reason the town has an atmosphere all of its own and this even applies to its buildings, which consist mainly of neat rows of officers' quarters.

[⌖] As with the majority of beaches on the mainland side of the Mar Menor the shoreline has been straightened, creating a narrow sandy beach which ends in a shelf at the water's edge. The water is very shallow.

[S] *Club Náutico.*

[🗝] *Urbanización Cuatro Picos.*

[🛈] Lo Pagán.

[🍴] *La Casona*, Ctra. de Pinatar; *La Parra*, Av. Sandoval; *Castilla*, Paseo Colón.

[🍷] *Six Brothers*, Playa; *Green*, Av. Torre Minguez.

[♪] *Don Diego*, Av. Sandoval.

[i] *Oficina Municipal de Turismo*, Paseo Colón; tel. (968) 57 11 16.

Beyond the San Javier airfield you come to the picturesque village of *Los Alcázares* which, like Santiago, has retained here and there the atmosphere of a seaside resort of the last century. A little to the south keep on the tiny road that follows the shore of the Mar Menor. Past Los Urrutias there is a succession of small pleasant beaches on this southern side of the inland sea, including *Los Nietos*, *Mar de Cristal* and *Playa Honda*.

La Manga del Mar Menor

The strip of land which separates the inland lake from the sea lies to the north of Playa Honda. It is 22 km long and between 100 and 800 m wide, and boasts a single hill. The scenery of La Manga is unique, with beaches that stretch for miles on both shores. It is a pity that so many buildings have been put up in such a great hurry on this sandy stretch. What used to be one of the most promising holiday regions in Spain has become one enormous development with no nucleus and with infrastructure problems. Much is being done, however, to rectify the faults of earlier years, and if you most enjoy watersports and spending your time on the beach you will be content here.

On the Mar Menor

 There are endless stretches of sand on both sides of La Manga. The Mar Menor beaches are, as would be expected, more protected than those on the Mediterranean side. In addition to the flat, endless sand there are several little coves at the foot of the solitary hill.

  Pedalos.

 Puerto Bello.

  S *Escuela Vela Luís Lerdo,* Hacienda Dos Mares.

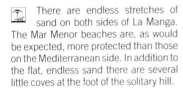 *Acuavanna,* Hotel Cavanna, Gran Vía s/n.

Q◌ *Escuela Tenis Dos Mares,* Hacienda Dos Mares; *Manga Sport,* Urbanización Los Alisios.

✓ *La Manga Country Club,* Los Belones (near La Manga; two 18-hole courses).

i. *Bowling Nuevas Sirenas,* Urbanización Nuevas Sirenas.

↰ *Parque Atracciones Dos Mares,* Hacienda Dos Mares; *Manga Park,* Nuevas Sirenas.

Go-Kart, Los Belones.

U At the Cabo de Palos.

66 *Red and Yellow,* Puerto Bello.

Casino del Mar Menor, Gran Vía.

Sancho Panza, El Algar; *Miramar,* Cabo de Palos; *Tropical,* Urbanización La Martinique.

San Remo, Plaza Bohemia; *Loro Verde,* Plaza Bohemia; *Mosqui,* Cabo de Palos.

Various establishments in the Plaza Bohemia and El Zoco.

Charlie Brown, Nueva Hacienda Dos Mares; *Gregory's,* Hacienda Dos Mares; *Baccará,* in the casino; *Vanity,* Eurovosa.

i *Centro de Iniciativas Turísticas,* Plaza Bohemia; tel. (968) 56 37 24.

South of the Cabo de Palos you reach the area given over to tourist development. Between the cape and Mazarrón (50 km) there is very little to see apart from a bleak, mountainous landscape, which has always been rich in mineral resources. Romans and Carthaginians dug for silver here, and during the last century the English found rich deposits of lead. In the centre of this strip of land lies *Cartagena* – the second Carthage. Cartagena cannot be described as a holiday resort and is mainly visited only for fiestas and ferias, which have their own attractions. If you want to go straight from the Mar Menor to Mazarrón it is probably best to bypass Cartagena on one of the small inland roads.

La Unión

La Unión came into being as a mining centre in 1868 and delights the connoisseur of Victorian architecture with its excellent works of art and buildings from that period. The town had its heyday at the turn of the century and was known throughout Spain as a kind of Eldorado.

Of particular interest are the *Edificio del Mercado* (market hall), an 'iron cathedral' of the industrial period, the *Casa de Piñón*, the *Ayuntamiento* (town hall), the *Rosario* church and the *hospital*. There are not many small towns in Europe whose principal buildings all represent the best, in stylistic terms, that the turn of the century produced.

Mid-August: *Festival del Cante de las Minas*, Festival of the Music of the Miners, a kind of flamenco. Famous Andalusian practitioners of the form appear in it.

Cartagena Pop. 180,000

The town lies in a deep-cut bay of the same name which narrows at its seaward end and is thus easy to defend from the land. Twice in its history this location has helped Cartagena to rise to an extraordinary position. The Carthaginians established New Carthage here in the 3rd c. B.C. and made it into the capital city of their Spanish colony. Subsequently Cartagena lay dormant, as it were, for a very long period, in fact right up to the 16th c. Then as Spain developed into a great naval power the town regained its

Cartagena

prominence. But the troubles of the 19th c., which culminated in defeat in the war against the USA in 1900, also brought with them the downfall of Cartagena as a naval base of the old imperial Spain. Finally the devastation brought about by the Civil War (1936–39) played its part in earning the run-down port the contemptuous label of the dreariest town in Spain.

In spite of that a brief visit can be interesting. From the ruins of the *Castillo de la Concepción* there is a good panoramic view over the town and the harbour, which is bordered by the *Paseo Alfonso XII* promenade. Also at the harbour is the *arsenal* which the first Bourbon kings built in the 18th c. In the *Plaza Héroes de Cavite* you will see a memorial to the heroes of the last two great naval battles fought by Spain against the USA, in Cavite (Philippines) and Santiago de Cuba. Both battles were lost and this finally brought about the decline both of Spain itself as a colonial and naval power, and of Cartagena as a port.

The two interesting museums in the town are concerned with archaeology, including, not surprisingly, marine archaeology. The *Museo Arqueológico*

Municipal in the Calle Ramón y Cajal contains finds from every period of the town's history. (Open: 10 a.m.–1 p.m., 4–6 p.m.; mornings only on Sundays, Mondays and public holidays.) In the more recent *Museo de Arqueología Marítima*, situated on the Quai Dique de Navidad at the harbour, you can see a fine collection of amphoras and other objects recovered from the sea. (Open: 10 a.m.–1 p.m., 5–7 p.m.; mornings only on Sundays, Mondays and public holidays.) Also to be seen is the *submarine 'Peral'* which is on show in the Paseo Alfonso XII. Designed by Isaac Peral Caballero, a native of Cartagena, the 22-m-long boat was launched in 1888. It was fitted with two 30-hp electro-motors and travelled at a speed of 8 knots.

Mazarrón

 Marisquería Bahía, c. Escorial; *Los Habaneros,* c. San Diego 60; *Mare Nostrum,* Paseo Alfonso XII.

Holy Week: grand processions in traditional costumes with processional figures carved by the Valencian sculptor Mariano Benlliure; July 25th: St James (Santiago), *Certamen Nacional del Trovo,* remarkable competitions between spontaneous rhymesters and poets; first half of November: international film festival of naval and sea films (*Semana del Cine Naval y del Mar*).

 Oficina Municipal de Turismo, Ayuntamiento; tel. (968) 50 64 83. *Centro de Iniciativas Turísticas,* c. Castellini 5; tel. (968) 50 75 49.

Mazarrón

The town itself lies 7 km from the sea. It is only over the past few years that tourist developments have sprung up around *Puerto de Mazarrón,* the little fishing village in the Bahía de Mazarrón. Some of these developments are quite attractive, others are quite obviously failures, even from an economic point of view. In any case the bay is over 10 km

long and consequently there is something for everybody. There is no lack of sandy beach between Puerto de Mazarrón and the *Punta de Azohía.*

To the west of the harbour the strange wind-sculpted rock formations of *Bolnuevo* (also called *Ciudad Encantada* – enchanted city) look down over one of the longest beaches in the locality. Beyond the harbour with its partly stony *Playa Grande* you will pass some sections of the beach which have been developed and others which are quite empty. At the end of the Bahía is the palm-lined beach *Playa de San Ginés,* below the neat houses of a tourist development.

Pedalos available on several sections of the beach.

 Club Náutico.

 Escuela de Vela Bahía de Mazarrón, Playa Negra.

 Polideportivo Municipal, Puerto; *Club de Tenis Playa Grande,* Playa de Castellar; *Club Playasol,* Urbanización Playasol 1; *Club Bahía,* Av. Costa Cálida.

 Jardin Carlos Muñoz, Puerto.

⊍ At the Vía Axial, Ordenación Bahía.

₺⸰ *Club Playa Grande,* Playa de Castellar; *Bolera La Isla,* Playa La Isla.

✕ *Miramar,* Playa La Isla; *Cumbre,* Urbanización La Cumbre; *Alborán,* Av. Concha Candau, Ordenación Bahía.

𝄞 *Domi Dos,* Edificio Costa Cálida, c. Carretera; *Puerto Distrito 7,* c. Francisco Yúfera.

♫ *Mundo Noche,* Vía Axial, Ordenación Bahía; *Le Galeon,* Ctra. Puerto Mazarrón.

ℹ *Oficina Municipal de Turismo,* c. San Hilario 24, Puerto de Mazarrón; tel. (968) 59 44 26.

The drive of about 50 km from the Bay of Mazarrón to Águilas is through a region which has nothing, apart from the two 'oases' of Mazarrón and Águilas themselves, of specific interest for the tourist. If you wish to have a look at this rural, undiscovered and wild part of Spain, which has hardly changed in the last fifty years, then approximately 15 km beyond Mazarrón turn left towards *Ramonete,* on to winding narrow mountain roads surfaced with gravel.

Ramonete

The smell is not exactly stimulating but it is typical of Murcia. Here, on endless covered plots, are grown (and manured!) the tomatoes which are sold in Great Britain out of season. The whole region concentrates on this crop. If you follow the road seawards you will come to the little fishing port of *Calnegre.* There are no moorings here; the boats are drawn up onto the attractive pebble beach. The village itself consists of just a few houses and a police station. Few tourists are ever seen here. A tortuously narrow gravel road leads from Ramonete over the *Sierra del Cantar*

which slopes steeply down to the sea between here and Águilas. From the highest point there is a unique view of the sea, of the rugged gloomy mountains, of the Cabo de Cope and of Mazarrón behind you. The road then leads down past a modern pilgrimage chapel (*Ermita de Cope*) into the plain of Águilas, and ends close to the *Playa de Calabardina,* a bay which is perhaps not quite as solitary as it used to be. From here there is a good road to Águilas.

Águilas

This dusty little town lies by the sea at the foot of barren mountains from which iron ore is extracted. In the 19th c. the English sought and found iron here, but little remains of that period of prosperity; old railway tracks, after emerging from the mine workings, end on huge unsteady landing-stages where the ships transporting the ore were loaded. Here and there is a dilapidated villa with an English air about it — but nothing else remains of the town's wealthy past. It was here too that the leather ball was first kicked around in Spain, as the British, of course, brought the game of football with them. Today Águilas makes its living from tomatoes, capers, fishing and tourism.

⌂ There is a promenade, with two beaches in front of a huge rock with an old watch-tower on top.

Águilas

Costa de Almería

Just a short distance to the south of Águilas you cross the provincial border between Murcia and Almería and enter Andalusia (Andalucía). Murcia forms a kind of corridor between on the one hand the regions of Valencia and Catalonia, which are stamped with the culture of the Mediterranean, and on the other Andalusia which for centuries was more oriental than European.

The scenery of the Costa de Almería is similar to that of Murcia. Here too until a few centuries ago there were large mines; as you drive along you will see gleaming hills of slate. The coastline is steep and mountainous yet the mountains open up here and there to reveal a sleepy little fishing village, a sandy beach a mile long, or a tiny green plain. In spite of the hilly nature of the countryside Almería makes a living chiefly from agriculture, especially greenhouse cultivation and early vegetables. Tourism is a new factor, and is of importance only to the west of the capital and port of Almería on the border with the Costa del Sol. The shores to the east and west of the Cabo de Gata are as yet undiscovered by mass tourism, and for the most part therefore undeveloped. In the region around Mojácar there are facilities of every type – beaches, sport, evening entertainment and excursions, but beyond this small stretch of coast the tourist has to be resourceful. If possible arrange to have the use of a car so that you can discover and enjoy every beautiful little corner along this coast.

The coast's emblem is the *Little Man of Indalo*. In his outstretched arms is a lucky rainbow which he holds over his head. This sign, which appears time and time again in cave paintings in Almería, was adopted as the symbol of a Mediterranean artists' movement in the forties and has since become the good-luck charm of Almería. Pendants bearing this symbol can be purchased everywhere.

The route now continues along the N-332 which in places turns inland. When this happens remain on a coastal road if there is one. Immediately after the provincial border you come to the beaches around *Los Terreros*, in small bays, sometimes sandy but often pebbly. Here and there are tiny holiday developments.

Beyond Los Terreros the N-332 bears away from the sea towards Cuevas del Almanzora, but you can remain close to the shore on a secondary road which fords the dry river-bed of the Rio Almanzora. Before you get to the river you skirt the foothills of the *Sierra Almagrera*, a mountain formation containing slate and ending quite abruptly at the sea. There are no beaches, just a lonely and strikingly harsh landscape.

The tourist area around Mojácar begins to the south of the Almanzora. The rugged mountains give way to gentle hills; long sandy beaches appear, with here and there campsites and developments. In the little fishing harbour of *Garrucha* a fish auction takes place at sunset but otherwise the town has nothing in particular to offer.

Mojácar

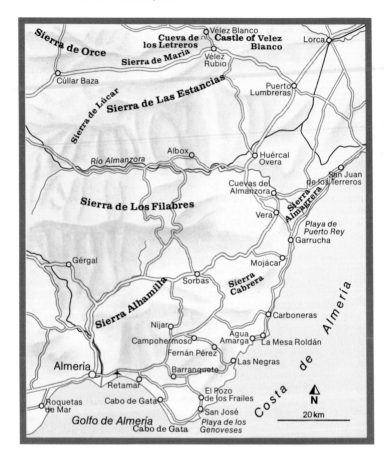

Mojácar Pop. 2500

This village nestles 2 km inland in the foothills of the Sierra Cabrera. Its character is typical of the villages in Almería: there is even more Arab influence here than in the rest of Andalusia. The houses which cling to the slopes of the hillside all have flat roofs and are constructed in terraces so that they virtually interlock, with narrow, bazaar-type winding alleys in between. You have the feeling you are walking on the roofs of the lower-lying houses. A

generation ago the women still wore yashmaks on certain occasions. Even the music which is played here, with its drawn-out half-tones, transports the listener into a world somewhere between Baghdad and Damascus.

There is another reason why Mojácar has an atmosphere entirely of its own. The droughts in the 19th c., the Civil War of 1936–39 and poverty in general forced the majority of the population to emigrate to South America or North Africa. At the beginning of the sixties the place was almost deserted. The local mayor then took the initiative and began to give away the dilapidated houses to prominent foreigners, on the condition that the buildings were restored. In 1966 Mojácar won a prize for being the most attractive village in Spain, and today it bubbles over with life, in the summer months at least. As well as local people a lot of foreigners, among them many artists, have set up home here. There is a succession of bars catering for every taste — from the dive with pounding music, for the wilder members of the younger generation, to the softly lit piano-bar.

During the day you can get a lot of enjoyment from just looking around the little shops; there are several resident jewellers and a hippy market like the one in Ibiza. Tour groups are accommodated in two very stylish hotels, one of which is situated up in the village and the other at the beach. Bus services between the village and the beach are good.

By the sea, as well as a Parador Nacional, there are various developments designed such that they blend perfectly with the local architecture. Special mention should be made of the *Pueblo-Indalo Complex* with its apartments, shops, bars and restaurants. Mojácar offers the tourist the opportunity — rare in Spain — of spending a holiday in charming surroundings away from concrete tower blocks, and of staying in a village which offers all the amenities found in large towns. Sports enthusiasts are also well catered for.

 The main beach of Mojácar, sandy but not very wide, extends from the Hotel Indalo in the south to the turning to the village itself. If you find it too crowded here then you can easily move further north or south. Fresh fish is obtainable from the *Chiringuitos*, the beach bars. You can also take a boat trip along the coast from Garrucha.

 Pedalos, water-scooters.

 Pueblo Indalo, Urbanización Los Angeles.

 Club de Golf Cortijo Grande on the AL-150 between Turre and Los Gallardos (18 holes).

 El Palacio, in the village; *Tito's*, Ctra. Indalo; *La Lubina*, Pueblo Indalo.

 Parador Nacional, Los Gauchos, at the beach; *Zoco Oriental* (Indonesian).

 Budú, c. Estación; *La Sartén*, c. Estación; *Pavana*, Glorieta; *Ninfas y Faunos*, Cruce de la Playa; *Coco Loco*, Ctra. Garrucha; *Pachá*, Ctra. Garrucha.

 Continental, Ctra. Garrucha; *Hollywood*, Guardia Vieja.

 Craftwork, hippy market, etc.; *Manitas*, jeweller, Plaza Nueva; *Pascal*.

ℹ️ *Centro de Iniciativas Turísticas,* Glorieta 3; *Oficina Municipal de Turismo,* Ayuntamiento.

🚌 Excursions from Mojácar

A drive into the hinterland from Mojácar takes you via Garrucha to the following places.

Vera, the chief town of the district, has a fortified *parish church* with a splendid Baroque altar which is well worth seeing. On sale you will find unglazed ceramics with Phoenician-looking patterns.

From Vera the N-340 leads to *Huércal Overa*, a fairly large town with a castle and a lovely church. In *Puerto Lumbreras* you bear left towards Granada and branch off in Vélez Rubio to Vélez Blanco.

Vélez Blanco (80 km).

The town is recognisable from afar by the silhouette of its castle, the *Castillo*

Vera

de los Fajardos, which was built in the 16th c. to defend the newly reconquered region from the Moors. The Marqués de los Vélez commissioned Italian builders and craftsmen to erect a castle appropriate to his rank. The result is magnificent; the combination of double merlons and the repeated arch motif in various sizes gives this building, which was erected primarily for military purposes, an unusually elegant appearance. Unfortunately the splendour is on the outside only – the famous marble inner courtyard, together with the rest of the interior decoration, was acquired by the Metropolitan Art Museum in New York. In spite of that the Castillo is one of the most original in Spain.

1 km outside the town is the *Cueva de los Letreros*, a cave with abstract paintings 4000 years old. You can also see a representation of the lucky *Indalo*, the rainbow man. (Enquire at the town hall about entry; tel. (951) 41 01 01.)

South of Mojácar the little coast road leads to the bay of *Carboneras* with a lovely sandy beach in front of the little fishing village. Continuing via Mesa Roldán you come to the pleasant sheltered beach of *Agua Amarga*; to travel further along the coast, however, you would need a four-wheel-drive vehicle. *Las Negras* is the only beach you can drive to along this stretch, and only from Níjar, via the farming villages of Campohermoso and Fernán Pérez. If

you bypass the rough hilly stretch of coast between Carboneras and the Cabo de Gata, by taking the AL-101 inland and joining the main N-332 road going south, after a few kilometres you can take a turning off to the right to *Níjar*. This regional centre, set in the middle of the richest agricultural land in Almería, is known for its ceramics and attractive handloom weaving. Do take time to watch the craftsmen at work and buy something to take home with you. About 8 km beyond the turning to Níjar you can drive via Barranquete and El Pozo de los Frailes to San José.

San José

This little town, which lies hidden away a short distance to the east of Cabo de Gata in a steeply sloping bay, has a few houses, a police station clinging to a rocky projection and a tiny but very good hotel restaurant. There is also a small beach here, and if you take the unmade road in the direction of the cape you come to unspoilt bays with sandy beaches which are among the finest in Spain — *Playa de los Genoveses* and *Playa de Monsul*.

   Hotel *San José;* terrace with a view over the bay.

Trop.

To get to the *Cabo de Gata* you go from San José either via the direct but unmade road, or round via El Pozo de los Frailes and Cortijada de Ruescas. The steep shoreline ends close to the cape with its lighthouse and salt workings. A long wide sandy beach stretches between here and Almería. You can only drive to this beach from the cape itself, however, or from the village of the same name. There are only rough tracks between this village and *Retamar*, where you will find an extensive development with hotels and restaurants, and all the usual facilities at the beach. From Almería you can drive westwards along the coast further into Andalusia.

Useful things to know

Before you go

Climate

Unlike the Atlantic north and north-west of Spain, the Andalusian region and the east coast have a Mediterranean climate. This means that on the east and south coasts autumn, winter and spring are decidedly mild with moderate humidity. In summer it is very hot during the day but cools off at night.

What to take

In the larger holiday resorts you will find just about everything you would normally need on holiday. Good sunglasses are indispensable. These can be bought locally but if you need special glasses or a particular suntan lotion, etc., it is advisable to take these with you. Photographers who need top-quality film should take an ample supply. A lens-hood and filters will probably be necessary. It is a good idea to take some reading matter with you.

First-aid kit. This is always useful on holiday and, although many preparations can be obtained in Spain, you should of course take with you any medicines which have been prescribed for you or which you regularly use at home.

Insurance

Spain, as a member of the EC, has a reciprocal agreement with Great Britain under which free medical treatment can be obtained for those entitled to it in their own country. To get this benefit it is essential to have form E.111, obtainable from the DSS (application forms at main post offices). In addition, however, you are strongly advised to take out holiday insurance with a reputable company. Most tour operators include this as part of their overall holiday package.

Getting to Eastern Spain

By air: Most visitors to Spain travel by air. There are regular services from London, with connecting flights from principal British and Irish airports, to the international airports of Barcelona, Valencia and Alicante. Many charter flights also operate to the principal holiday areas. The average journey time from London is 2 to 3 hours.

By rail: The journey from London via Paris to Valencia takes about 17 hours and to Alicante a further 3 hours. A change of train is necessary at either Port Bou or Barcelona. Sleepers and couchettes are available and there is a motorail service through France.

By road: It is a very long way from Great Britain to Eastern Spain — more than 2000 km — but the time spent behind the wheel can be shortened by making use of one of the motorail services through France.

By sea: There are no regular services to Eastern Spain but it is possible to use the Brittany Ferries service from Plymouth to Santander on the north coast of Spain.

Immigration and customs regulations

A passport is all that is required for a stay in Spain of up to three months. Should you wish to spend longer a visa will be necessary. Please note, however, that you should have your passport stamped at the border, and if occasion should arise produce evidence to the police of your date of arrival. In order to take your car into Spain it is essential to have your driving licence, and the green insurance card is advisable. Under no circumstances allow a Spanish citizen (domiciled in Spain) to drive your car as this is a customs offence and could result in the loss of the car.

Following the entry of Spain into the EC British visitors now enjoy the more generous EC customs allowances: 300 cigarettes or 75 cigars or 400 grammes of tobacco; 1.5 litres of spirits (over 22% alcohol) or 3 litres of sparkling or fortified wine; and 5 litres of other wine. If any or all of these goods have been bought at a duty-free shop, or on a ship or aircraft, the permitted quantities are approximately two-thirds of those given above. Other goods and souvenirs up to a value of £250 are also allowed in duty-free.

There are no limits to the amount of Spanish or foreign currency which may be brought in, but large amounts should be declared on arrival to avoid possible difficulty when leaving the country. Up to 100,000 pesetas may be taken out.

During your stay
Camping

Camping sites appear everywhere along the coast. A useful publication is the Official Camping Guide which may be obtained from the Spanish National Tourist Office in London (see page 94). Sites are state run and divided into categories. Casual camping is not welcomed in Spain and in summer is strictly forbidden because of the fire risk. This rule also applies to caravans.

Currency and banks

The Spanish unit of currency is the *peseta*, abbreviated to pta. and pts. or ptas. (plural). Coins and notes are in denominations of 1, 5, 10, 25, 50, 100 and 500 ptas. and 100, 200, 500, 1000, 2000, 5000 and 10,000 ptas. respectively. The *duro* is a colloquial term for 5 ptas. The rate of exchange fluctuates frequently and should be checked at a bank. It is worth comparing the rates of exchange, as travel agencies and savings banks usually offer less favourable rates than banks. Eurocheques are becoming more widely accepted now that Spain has joined the EC and you should have no difficulty using them in hotels and shops.

Electricity

Most of the country has now been converted to 220 volts, but occasionally you may come across 110 volts.

Newspapers and books

Most British newspapers are on sale in the major Spanish resorts. Paperbacks in English can also be obtained but the choice is somewhat limited.

Opening times
Churches

If you are planning to visit a town which has churches you particularly wish to see, do enquire beforehand about the opening times. There have been so many art thefts from Spanish churches in recent years that they no longer keep their doors open all day long. You can, however, expect most large churches to be open from 8–11 a.m. and from 6–8 p.m. for public worship.

Museums

Wherever possible opening times have been given but they do, of course, change slightly from year to year. Generally, museums open from 9 a.m.– 1 p.m. on weekdays and some open again from 4–7 p.m.; the exception is Monday when practically all museums are closed. At weekends times vary.

Shops and banks

The traditional Spanish siesta taken after lunch determines business hours and that explains why opening times seem so strange to us — from 9 a.m.– 1 p.m. and from 5–8 p.m., although many shops, especially those in the large tourist towns which sell souvenirs and newspapers, remain open until midnight. Banks are usually open from 9 a.m.–2 p.m.

Paradors

Paradores Nacionales de Turismo can be found in many resorts. These are good-class hotels, often occupying old castles, country houses and monasteries, and offer very high standards of accommodation and cuisine.

Post

Post offices *(Correo)* are open from 9 a.m.–2 p.m. and in the afternoon for the sale of stamps only. These may also be obtained from tobacconists *(Estanco)*. You will recognise these shops either by the red-yellow-red of the national colours, or by a stylised letter 'T' on a tobacco leaf. Mail can be sent to the *Lista de Correos* (Poste Restante) at any post office.

Telephone

The telephone service in Spain is independent of the postal services. In provincial capitals and in tourist resorts there are telephone offices *(Telefónica* or *Locutorio Público),* and everywhere you will find telephone kiosks from which you can make international calls direct using 25 and 100 ptas. coins. The telephone code from Spain to Great Britain is 07 44.

Tipping

As in all Mediterranean countries tips *(propinas)* are expected in Spain and gladly received. In addition a tip must be given willingly! Take no notice of the phrase *servicio incluido* (service included) as this is always misleading. Taxi-drivers, hairdressers, shoe-cleaners and particularly waiters should be given a propina of 10% of the bill. When giving a tip bear in mind the following: first pay the bill, then hand over the tip after receiving the change, or leave it on the table or bar. To create a good impression at your hotel, make a 'part-payment' at the end of each week; 500 ptas. is certainly not too much if you are satisfied with the service. By so doing, you are not only showing your appreciation but also establishing a direct relationship with the person receiving the tip.

Tobacco and cigarettes

These may be purchased either at the Estanco, the tobacconist's shop with the red-yellow-red of the Spanish colours on the door or a sign depicting a 'T' on a tobacco leaf, or in any bar. *Kioscos* also sell everything from newspapers and ball-point pens to tobacco and chewing-gum. The usual international brands of cigarettes and tobacco are considerably cheaper than in the U.K. Spanish brands are very good and cheap. Pale tobacco: Fortuna and Fortuna Lights (American type) or Royal Crown (English type). Dark tobacco is the best in Europe: Habanos (very strong), Ducados, Coronas and Rex (light). The prices of the Spanish brands vary between 50 and 200 ptas. Cigars from Cuba and the Canary Islands are good value and of a high quality. Pipe tobacco is manufactured under licence or is imported.

Traffic regulations

The wearing of seat belts is compulsory in Spain but not within city limits. The limit of alcohol in the blood is 0.08%. The speed limit in built-up areas is 60 km p.h.; outside built-up areas it varies between 90 and 100 km p.h. On motorways the limit is 120 km p.h. For the purpose of overtaking, the limits are raised by 20 km p.h. Cars towing trailers or caravans are limited to 80 km p.h. on dual carriageways and motorways and to 70 km p.h. on roads outside built-up areas. Overtaking regulations must be strictly adhered to: observe all signs, and markings on the road itself, and when overtaking use indicators and sound the horn by day (flash headlights at night). Traffic is kept under surveillance by the *Guardia Civil de Tráfico.* If fines are not paid on the spot the vehicle may be confiscated. It pays to have a friendly and polite attitude towards the police who are always very willing to help in emergencies.

Transport in Spain

Buses are widely used in Spain and are usually operated by private firms who provide services to almost all the places mentioned in this guide. Timetables can be obtained from Tourist Information Offices (*Oficinas de Información de Turismo*; see below).

Car hire: Cars may be hired from well known and not so well known firms in all main towns and tourist resorts. The smaller firms frequently offer more favourable terms, but it is very important to pay a little extra for fully comprehensive insurance cover. Regular-grade petrol (92 octane) and super-grade (97 octane) are available. Spain, like other EC countries, must have unleaded petrol (95 octane) on sale. All petrol stations are open from 7 a.m. to 11 p.m. and many are open throughout the night. They are, however, under no obligation to give change during the night.

The highway system in Spain is generally well maintained and well signposted. Only in Murcia and Almería is it not quite up to standard. The main arterial road for travel within the region covered by this guide is the relatively uncrowded *Autopista de Peaje* (toll road), which extends from the French border close to La Jonquera to beyond Alicante. It is not worth using the road which runs parallel to it, the *Carretera Nacional*, on long stretches as it is crowded with lorries avoiding tolls.

Railways: The Spanish railway system, RENFE, is quite extensive. Most lines are broad-gauge and although mainline services are good, local trains tend to be rather slow.

Taxis: Fares are reasonable but depend on the zone and the time of day. If the taxi has a meter make sure it is working before starting your journey. For cross-country journeys it is advisable to agree a price with the driver beforehand.

Safety abroad

It is unfortunately true that petty crime (stealing from cars, picking of pockets, snatching of handbags and other forms of pilfering) is today a regrettable fact of life in the majority of countries. When on holiday you should take all possible steps to avoid becoming a victim of the opportunist thief. Insurance of money and baggage is strongly recommended. Do not carry large sums of money or valuables on your person. These can usually be deposited in a safe in your hotel. Women should not wear valuable jewellery, and handbags should be carried on the inside arm when walking on the pavement. Men should not carry a wallet in a hip pocket. Do not leave any valuables on view in a car. Cars are very rarely stolen — they are only relieved of their contents. Do not park at night in an unlit street but look for a busy spot, or best of all put the car in a secure car park or garage. Should you run into difficulties go to the *Comisaría de Policía* in the city (not to the *Policía Municipal*) or to the *Guardia Civil* if you are in the country.

Important addresses
Diplomatic and consular offices
British Embassy
Calle de Fernando el Santo 16, Madrid; tel. (91) 4 19 02 00.
British Consulates
Plaza Calvo Sotelo 1-2 (1st floor), Alicante; tel. (965) 21 61 90.
Calle Real 33, Tarragona; tel. (0977) 22 08 12.

Airlines
British Airways
Explanada de España 3, Alicante; tel. (965) 20 05 94.
Edificio Banco de Londres, Plaza Rodrigo Botet 6, Valencia; tel. (96) 3 21 50 21.

Tourist Information Offices
Spanish National Tourist Office
57-58 St James's Street
London SW1A 1LD; tel. (071) 499 0901.
In Spain there are *Jefaturas Provinciales de Turismo* in provincial capitals and *Oficinas de Información de Turismo* in major towns.

Useful words and phrases

Although English is widely understood in those parts of Spain which are frequented by tourists, the visitor will undoubtedly find a few words and phrases of Spanish very useful. In general pronunciation is not too difficult; *ñ* sounds very like the *ni* in *onion*; *x* and *c* before *e* and *i* are usually lisped; a final *d* generally becomes *th* (as in *thin*) and a medial *d* like *th* in *the*. The letters *ll* should be pronounced as if they were *ly* or in some places *y*. A word ending in a vowel or in *n* or *s* is normally stressed on the last syllable but one; a word ending in any other consonant on the final syllable. Any exceptions bear an acute accent on the stressed syllable.

please	¡ por favor !	0 cero
thank you (very much)	¡ (muchas) gracias !	1 un(o)
yes / no	sí / no	2 dos
excuse me	¡ con permiso !	3 tres
do you speak English ?	¿ habla Usted inglés ?	4 cuatro
I do not understand	no entiendo	5 cinco
good morning	¡ Buenos días !	6 seis
good afternoon	¡ Buenas tardes !	7 siete
good night	¡ Buenas noches !	8 ocho
goodbye	¡ Adiós !	9 nueve
how much is it?	¿ qué precio tiene ?	10 diez
I should like	quisiera	11 once
a room with private bath	un habitación con baño	12 doce
the bill, please!	¡ la cuenta (la nota) por favor !	20 veinte
everything included	todo incluido	50 cincuenta
when is it open ?	¿ a qué hora está abierto ?	100 ciento
when is it shut ?	¿ a qué hora se cierra ?	
where is ..... street ?	¿ dónde está la Calle......?	
the road to.... ?	el camino para ..... ?	
how far ?	¿ qué distancia ?	
to the left / right	a la izquierda / direcha	
straight on	siempre derecho	
post office	correo	
railway station	estación	
town hall	ayuntamiento	
exchange office	cambio	
police station	comisaría	
public telephone	teléfono público	
Tourist Information Office	Oficina de Información de Turismo	
doctor	médico	
chemist	farmacia	
toilet	retrete	
ladies	señoras	
gentlemen	señores	
engaged	ocupado	
free	libre	
entrance	entrada	
exit	salida	
today / tomorrow	hoy / mañana	
Sunday / Monday	domingo / lunes	
Tuesday / Wednesday	martes / miércoles	
Thursday / Friday	jueves / viernes	
Saturday / holiday	sábado / día festivo	

Index